Manifest Your Mate

a journey for attraction

by
Joan Severance

Distributed by Ingram Book Company worldwide.

Take Two Imprints books may be order through booksellers. For autographed copies contact publisher or purchase through website:

Take Two Imprints
5300 N. Braeswood Blvd.4 - 421
Houston, TX 77096
www.taketwoimprints.com
contact@taketwoimprints.com

Cover Image by gyva grafika via colourbox.com
Cover Designs & *Graphics* by Cher Schmitt

The author's intent is to provide information to assist you on your quest. The publisher and author assume no responsibility that the reader will achieve the same experiences or outcomes as described here within. The views presented in this book are solely that of the author. The publisher and author do not dispense medical advice and the contents of this book are not to be used as treatment for medical, psychological or emotional concerns without a physician's supervision.

Severance, Joan
Manifest Your Mate: a journey for attraction / Joan Severance
1.Relationships: Dating, Love and Romance 2. Self-Help 3. Self-Transformation

ISBN: 978-0-9988615-0-0   6 x 9 Perfect Bound Softcover

This book is dedicated to all women who are seeking that special man to share the experience of life. To those who are curious about the power that resides in their heart. To those who know the power of their mind and to those who decide to step on the conscious path of co-creation.

Contents

Part Three – It's about TIME

Foreword

Like so many of my female friends, I am single after a few marriages, home schooling four kids, and in my fifties. Although I love my life, my children and what I have accomplished thus far, I do seek a man in my life because I love being in love. I love being adored. I love being touched by a man I am in love with. I love the special space created when I am in love with a man.

In *Manifest Your Mate*, my friend, Joan Severance has created a process and a place for anyone to use who truly seeks the man of their dreams. Although the process may feel foreign to many, it works. The chapters walk you through the journey of creating your perfect mate. Using your imagination, specific details, dreams, focused intent and inner inquisition you bring to life the one you seek. Then in a fun way you send it to the Universe with the Universal Command Form, so that it gets delivered to your life. Be careful what you wish for. My experience had me swatting men away like flies from the start.

When I first met Joan, I needed some guidance to help me with a legal battle I was going through. We met for breakfast with some other friends of mine and she listened to my frantic story. Then she simply said, "What is it you want to have as the outcome and when do you want it to happen by?

Never thinking that I could create my outcome in this situation I was taken aback by the question. Flustered and confused. She quickly recounted a story of her own awakening to the fact that we are co-creators. After listening to her story, she had me write on a napkin my exact desire regarding the situation. She told me not to bother with the "how" of the outcome, but rather stick to what I had written and "know" that it would happen exactly that way, no matter what obstacles seemed to appear.

When I was approached for the *12 Women 12 Weeks to Manifest Your Mate* study I was cynical and had unrealistic expectations of a mate. I thought I had to settle for something less than I wanted because that is all that I was attracting to myself, at the time. I realized that I had given up and resolved to being alone for the rest of my life. *Manifest Your Mate* came just at the right time for me. Encouraged by the success I had with my legal issue after implementing and sticking to my desired outcome - what Joan showed me - the prospect of manifesting a mate in the same way was intriguing. The past year showed me that I am a major contributor to the outcome of the events and turning points in my life that have occurred.

Focusing on what I want instead of what I don't want brought crisp clear images the minute I would close my eyes. Writing down exactly what I wanted in a man from the physical, emotional, professional, family aspects and more, gave me a place to read my thoughts and edit my desires as I worked through the book. Creating a clearer image of the man of my dreams.

Some with a specific trait that I had carefully noted in the journal. One such trait was someone who was musically inclined. The next day a man appeared in my life with that trait plus many others I had noted. I got excited by that gift and then I got more specific, because he wasn't the guy for me. I went back to the journal and erased - musically inclined - and wrote I wanted an actual musician. Then he appeared as well.

The *Take a Moment Take a Breath* pause in each chapter made me realize that all things are possible I just had to open-up and be more specific about the qualities I wanted in a man. As I was looking inward to search for them I started realizing certain qualities I sought in another were not residing in me. I had not developed them within myself. I realized I needed to identify and work on those qualities personally before they could appear externally. If I wanted them in my mate wouldn't he deserve the same level of evolvement?

I tried to dream up my soul-mate and then started focusing on who I wanted to be as an individual. How could I share a better me with a soul-mate? I was surprised at how the principles in *Manifest Your Mate* worked. By looking inward, I found a soul-mate within myself. The *What Your Dreams Say* pages helped me keep track of what was going on within me at a higher level. The *Meaningful Triggers* area got quite full with past stuff that came up. Thank you for including space to write all the questions that came up within me in the *Notes and Questions* area. To have all this in one journal has allowed me to edit along the process. Yes, using a pencil and a giant eraser was a fabulous suggestion.

I feel whole on my own now and not in need of someone else to have complete fulfillment. I am a much more evolved human being and my capacity for love has deepened. I now have a better understanding about what I really want and I feel confident in what I must offer a mate.

Manifest Your Mate worked in ways I did not expect. It worked deeper than I had imagined. The principles you outlined are a powerful force and I am now carefully and enthusiastically applying them to manifest other things in my life, including a special mate to share my extraordinary journey.

Thank you, my friend, for teaching me profound thinking patterns that have proven miraculous and that have enlightened and empowered me. The principles in *Manifest Your Mate* have sent me in such a positive direction and have significantly enriched my life!

Cynthia Garrett
Mom and Real Estate Developer
Sedona, AZ

Preface

In the beginning, God created the Heavens and the Earth. Then He/ She said "Let there be light" and there was light.

STOP!!!!

Have you ever stopped to think about that second sentence for a moment? That is powerful stuff!! It was said and it happened! Forget religion in the above-mentioned statement, instead focus on the actions.

Expression equals instant reality.

It was said and it happened. Forget that maybe that wasn't quite how it happened. Instead, focus on the thought of what would happen if it was that simple. While reading this book, and answering the questions in it, it is essential to be open to believe that it happens this way.

Imagine if we all had that same capacity. What we express becomes reality. Hashnu O'Hara, possibly a pseudonym for the author William Walker Atkinson, the pioneer of the New Thought movement, states: "Thought rays sent out through the ether with direct force will return upon their center with equal force to that which sent them forth. So, according to this law, thought goes out, charged with its duty, and returns to the starting point having fulfilled its mission."

My interpretation is that thought creates your reality or what you wish for you will get. The stronger the intent of the thought, desire or wish the clearer and more exact match will appear or happen.

In many ways, it does and we never see it happening. You may say to yourself, *I'm not good at sports,* and you are not. Every attempt you make you prove it to yourself over and over, by failing at the sport. Eventually giving up in frustration with —*I was never any good at sports anyway.* This is a negative example, of course, but most of us are programmed negatively.

Let's take another example. *I will never find Mr. Perfect, so I must settle for Mr. Maybe.* So, you settle, never giving Mr. Perfect the opportunity to find you.

If expression equals instant reality, then why can't you get exactly what it is you want?

Here is something else to ponder. Have you ever been in your house just doing the usual and suddenly you think of someone who has not popped into your mind for some time? You may think, *I wonder how they are doing. I should give them a call or drop them a note. It would be great to see them or talk to them.* Then to your utter amazement they contact you via the phone, mail, e-mail or you run into them somewhere and they say they were just thinking of you also. Coincidence? Or, expression equals reality. I feel coincidences are coinciding events that are heading towards each other. The mere thought, feeling or intent sent in a specific direction alerts and attracts the recipient. Initiating movement back toward the source of the thought. It happens in nanoseconds. Something to think about as you use *Manifest Your Mate.*

Preface

Why can't you get exactly what it is you want? Maybe because you don't really know what it is you want. You probably have very clear ideas of what you don't want. You might have vague ideas, but not specific ones of what you want.

Tall, dark and handsome is very vague—and would deliver millions of men to your door. A more specific statement would be: I want to meet someone who is 6' 2", slender athletic build, light brown skin, blue eyes and resembles Brad Pitt, has Will Smith's smile, and Jack Black's humor. That statement narrows down the order a bit. As you get more and more specific about who you want to attract to you, you will see that these people will appear in your life in miraculous ways.

Imagine the Universe as a big bank in the sky. It has only three types of deposit/withdrawal slips to be filled out: Definitely, Maybe and Definitely Not. This bank has a quicker and easier way for you to do your banking. Faster than an ATM or online banking. It uses your words! Whether spoken, thought or written. The bank will give you what you request. Based on certain specific criteria you enter on the slips—dates, traits, amounts—you may receive your request immediately. So being very specific on the proper Universal slip is the first important step when doing business with this institution.

This book allows you to see where you are not specific enough in your requests. It creates space for you to detail and express, within a serious but light-hearted format.

The Law of Attraction does work. There are many books on this subject. The big one I remember is the Bible with—*Ask and you shall receive.* So why don't we believe this or use it to our advantage every minute of the day?

My open mind and curiosity, when it comes to unknown and unseen forces, led me to a man named Boaz Rauchwerger. His

31-Day Charge program is the first thing I did in my search for the powers that guide this Law of Attraction. Every day for 31 day or whatever the month holds, upon waking, I would listen to his advice for that day then try to practice it.

At the end of the *31 Day Charge* I sat down and wrote a decree stating what I wanted. I stated my name and desire. In this instance, it was for a certain dollar amount to be a spokesperson for any product. I gave a deadline for the delivery of my desire. Almost immediately a friend said he knew of someone looking for a spokesperson for their skin care line. Happily, I suggested to receive something in writing.

Twenty-seven days later I received a letter in the mail from the person that my friend had put me in contact with. The letter was an offer. The offer was for the exact amount and position that I had put in my decree. My mouth fell agape. I smiled from ear to ear. I couldn't stop laughing at the simplicity and orchestration of what had transpired over the last thirty days. Surrounding myself with the knowledge of this power I knew existed, I sat back filled with gratitude. From now on I had to be cautious with my thoughts.

This all sounds too good to be true, doesn't it? Well, my first attempt delivered exactly what I asked for but did not deliver the money. In my decree, I had only asked for the offer. I wasn't specific enough to put that I would sign a contract, perform the work and receive payment.

The idea for this book came about after I had a bad car accident. I was in the middle of a six-lane road, in the suicide lane—I now know why it is called that. I was about to turn left across three lanes of oncoming traffic. A few things were happening at the same time with me:

- My car was up for sale and I was happy to be going to the dealer to sell back my car. I was on my way to the gym, which is why I was turning left.
- I had just finished reading a book in French, *La principle du LOLA* [2] by Rene Egli (the English version is The LOLA Principle), about how thought creates reality. If you have ever read a book in a language that you are not fluent in then you know how you must concentrate, use a dictionary and reread almost every word.
- I was excited to finally sell my car. I had one too many at that moment and was downsizing my collection.

So, sitting in that lane, a thought flashed across my mind. I mean this was one of those split-second things that doesn't even matter, or so we think. How many of these do you have in a day?

Here is the fleeting thought:

I can't wait to get rid of my car.

As simple as that and as quick as that. It had a very happy connotation attached to it as well. Then, the oncoming traffic allowed for me to finally make that left turn, so I stepped on the gas and turned to get to the gym.

Suddenly everything went white. When the white went away I found myself with the passenger seat smashed up against the right side of my body, glass everywhere and looking straight into a coffee shop at an odd angle. I slowly started processing the information lying around me. The expressions on the two cops that were rushing to me made it clear that something must have happened.

It did!

The Universe listened to my demand and took care of business in the most efficient and expeditious way it could, by having someone smash into my car.

I *can't wait* to get rid of my car, was taken literally and instantaneously by the Universe.

A tow truck and ambulance arrived within minutes. The cops cut my seat belt and told me not to move. I realized I had been sideswiped and my car was now totaled. I also felt my left knee smashed between the door and steering wheel and looked to see a bruise starting to form. The nice cops asked if was hurt in any way. It was at this moment that I made a conscious decision about my reality.

If the Universe answered this tiny thought instantaneously, then I had a choice right now to declare that I was not injured, had no pain and would walk away from this totally fine. So, that is just what I did. A huge smile creeped across my face.

Trying to stay focused, I answered the young cop. "I am perfectly fine. You don't know how fine, officer."

He looked at me as if I were drunk, stoned or high on something. He then asked, "Have you been drinking?"

Of which I of course replied, "No," with an even bigger smile. The paramedic insisted I sign a paper if I was not going to the emergency room. So, I did. The tow truck had my car up on the flatbed so fast I was in shock. They sped off to some unknown lot within seconds.

The man who smashed into me had gotten out of his car with no problem and came to see if I was all right. Amazingly he was completely unharmed and his car barely damaged. *Hmmm!* How could his car not be damaged, when he slammed into the side of mine? These questions made it clear to me that there was a Higher Power that was playing with me at that moment. One that understood the urgency of the words—*can't wait!*

I stood there choosing to create my reality. I had just gotten rid of my car by having a fleeting thought. Now I could decide what physical effect this would have on me. I simply thought to myself, *I am not hurt nor in any pain.* That is what happened. The bruise was gone by that evening. There was no soreness. No whiplash either. I was high on life and my sudden discovery of how the universe works. I didn't tell anyone about this accident until years later.

In retrospect, I had not been specific enough on that demand, but of course, I really had no clue that a fleeting thought was a demand or that instant delivery of a wish could possibly happen. When I think back upon the car that smashed into mine, the car and man had no damage or injuries. The police were right there in the coffee shop. The ambulance around the corner. The stage was perfectly set for that scene to occur. I believe all those people were angels that got delivered to fulfill my demand—my fleeting thought.

This workbook is a great tool and storage device as you set out to create the perfect mate. Attracting them to you with thoughts, actions and emotions you express in this journal, will broadcast across the globe your intended desires.

Don't be amazed if once you get going with this you find yourself changing jobs, countries and friends. You may start new activities, join groups and/or relocate. The Universe will use what it can to get you together with your created mate. All those around you may suddenly become players in this huge ordeal. Like in the movie *The Game,* starring Michael Douglas and Sean Penn. If you haven't seen it, I won't spoil it for you.

So, keep your eyes, mind and heart open to all the wonderful possibilities that exist for you to create a mate with the laws of attraction. It might become quite clear to you that we are all angels to someone along the path of life.

How To Use This Book

To those who are truly seeking a mate, partner for life, husband, or next deep relationship, these pages will assist in bringing that person into your life through creatively visualizing, writing down your desires and believing them into your life.

This book is used as an artist would use a canvas, a writer would use paper and a sculpture would use clay. It is for the creation process of designing the man you wish to bring into your life. It is not for mirroring a man into your life so you can work out your issues. There are plenty of other books on the market that will help you in that endeavor. It is not about you! It's about him—the person your creative loving heart is seeking.

If you build it, they will come, is like the line from *Field of Dreams* with Kevin Costner. His character believed that if he built a baseball field that a legendary player would come to it. In the movie, of course that actually happens. Belief is key when it comes to certain things happening or not. For instance, the placebo effect is when someone believes they are taking medicine that will cure them of their ailment and they get cured, even though the medicine was a sugar pill. Obviously, the pill did not cure them of anything, it was solely their belief that it would.

Do you believe your thoughts are felt? Do you think they can travel outside of your body? According to Tim Welsh, a professor of Kinesiology at the University of Toronto, a thought can be generated and acted upon in the body within 150 milliseconds. That's fast! So, if it doesn't have to have a reaction within the body, how fast is a thought? I think thoughts are instant. Possibly they speed along waveforms like light or sound. A thought is like a text, once you push send, it is there in a split second, or faster.

We pray or meditate for and on many things. Consider this the same practice only in a journal format. You will create your mate by answering questions, filling in blanks and using your imagination to *see* and *feel* who he is before you actually meet him. It's fun and it works because all thought is the initiator of reality.

Thoughts are felt. Remember when you did something wrong as a child and your parent looked at you without saying a word. You knew what they were thinking. You felt what they were expressing. Words were not necessary. If you have had the joy of looking into the eyes of someone you love and they expressed love back to you in theirs, you know that thoughts are felt. Not only felt on an emotional level but on a physical level. Instantly you experience change at your cellular level due to hormones and neurotransmitters. So, thoughts are powerful things.

Every thought gives off a signal and attracts to it a similar signal. It's like those toy guns with the suction cups on the ends of the darts. The thought is the dart. The dart hits your desire (target). You then retrieve the dart with the desire stuck to it. So be careful what you wish for.

Take your time to work through the book. Don't rush and expect that by the end of the week your mate will arrive. Set an achievable deadline for your delivery, one that fits your schedule. Are you really ready, right now? Or, are you building a business and have no time. Are you focused on a million other things? Are you dealing with an illness? A death? Self-doubt? At any time after you start this process you feel you are not ready, simply stop and revisit it at a later date.

When you are ready, pick it up again. By narrowing down the physical, emotional and psychological aspects that you wish your new mate to have, you are creating a two-way path of expression. You can zero in on them and them on you.

For instance, if you pray to have a tall dark handsome man in your life, you have just sent a Universal Order. The Universe looks at this order and can't begin to process it because it is so broad. By the way, the Universe states that everyone is beautiful and handsome. There are millions of people who fit that description. So, the order may never get filled in your lifetime. Remember always, the Universe is here to serve and wishes to do so. With millions of people placing orders every second it must get overwhelmed at times and that is why being very specific is a must when trying to bring *Mr. Right* into your life.

Here is an example of a Universal Order:

"Can I get your full name please?" the Universal server person asked.

"Joan Severance," I replied.

"Can I take your order please?" they continued.

"Yes, uh, I will have a 6'4" male about 200 lbs., with longish sandy hair, plump medium-sized lips, athletic build, no tendency towards being overweight, 12.5 shoe size, sharply dressed, likes boxers over briefs. He has a great smile and is extroverted. And....uh, oh yeah, and single!" I said giggling.

"Can I get you any sides with that order?" they questioned.

I answered, "Um…yes, please. He's more spiritual than religious, well read, educated, comes from a rock-solid family, has at least one sister and one brother, owns his own place, owns his own car."

"Anything else?" they requested.

"Well, uh, he has about 75,000-200,000 in the bank in cash, a great credit score, loves his profession, looking to settle down with a female like me. He likes pets, likes museums, likes to travel," I excitedly said.

"Would you like any condiments with that?" they asked.

"Hmmm! Yeah! I would. Thanks for asking. How about…he gives a great massage! He loves to cook and clean. He's romantic and treats me like a queen. He is very compassionate and typically happy. Oh… and he fits in my car," I laughed.

"How do you feel knowing he is on his way?" they responded.

"Really!!!?? You have that?? Wow! Uh…so, thankful. I feel exuberant. Happy. Grateful! Thank so much!" I replied as I jumped up and down with joy and started texting all my girlfriends.

"Okay, your order will be ready in about 5 minutes. If you would like to go pull yourself together, we have a mirror in the restroom. You can pick your order up in that line over there."

The following sections guide you to write, think, meditate, feel and create a place for you to express.

Mental Moment

Concentration and focus always helps bring what we seek into vision and with this technique into reality or at least a lot closer. It's sort of a relaxing thing to do anyway. It blows out the dust and debris of other thoughts and allows space for the new information about your mate to find its place in consciousness and your heart, a must for creating your mate.

This can be accomplished anywhere but best when you will not be disturbed and have some time to write in the journal right afterwards. Maybe in the morning when you wake up, at lunch in a park or just before you go to bed, like a prayer would be done.

Take a deep breath in and exhale out all the way and then exhale even more. Then breathe in all the way. And then a little more. Do this at least three times. Each time you breathe in, imagine you are bringing in extra light sparkling dots and exhale as if you are blowing out old cobwebs and dust. Visualize the things you wish to clear out being blown out of your nostrils and/or mouth and imagine light filling you up and replacing the *old dust* you removed.

Think of something that makes you happy. When you get that feeling, smile. When you smile, take that feeling and focus it in the area of your heart. Notice how good you feel. From this *good feeling* send a message of love to all those you know. Now breathe in and imagine that each person received that message. Now send the feeling of love to everyone in the world and know that they received it. Breathe in once more and exhale to a calm, relaxed space in your heart. You are ready to *ask and receive* now that your heart is happy.

This should set a good vibration in your conscience, allow the Universe to bring info to you and for clear thinking of what you want in a mate. Cast your desire and take note of any information that comes your way. Try not to direct the info, decipher or analyze. Just take note of the information, no matter how strange it may seem to you. Write it down.

My Mate Statements

This is a place for you to start. Simply circle and/or write in what you want in your mate. Circle as many traits as you wish or as few. There is a space for you to write in some things if your desired traits are not listed or if you think of other traits you feel represent what he will be. These sections are to spark awareness about what you want. Expand and embellish and dare to dream him into being.

Different sections provide ample space for you to create your mate. Use a pencil, as you may need to narrow things down over time. You may come back to any one of these sections after you have completed the book. As things change inside yourself and as your opportunities broaden, your desires may start to become more clear. Skip over a chapter if you prefer to start with another set of traits. Make sure that you are not changing your desires to fit someone you met. Stay true to your intent.

Meaningful Memories or Triggers

We have all had moments in our life that we cherish and can recall almost instantly. A fond memory of the touch of a hand across your back from a lover. A vacation that was perfect. Hearing your Dad say he loved you as he tucked you into bed. Even words in a letter received from a close friend that helped you through hard times. These moments usually cause pleasant feelings in our body. We may also experience a trigger—unpleasantness or agitation—causing a negative feeling, thought or reaction. This section is for you to place any meaningful memories or triggers that are recalled during the process of manifesting your mate.

These can be anything that comes up. The exercise is to find the meaning in the experience or feelings that you had then or now, in the recall of them. Has there been a change in your attitude that you are aware of and if so what is it? Has this change guided you to better and healthier relationships with yourself, friends, family and lovers? If no change has occurred, you may wish to make a note. Is a trigger from a past circumstance creating your current feeling? Could it or does it hinder you in any way?

If a trigger or memory stirs great emotion in you, so much that you cannot complete the workbook, take a break! Meditate on the trigger and emotion. Ask for guidance as to where it comes from, why it is triggering you, how to transform the negative feelings into positive ones and transmute the trigger. When you connect with joy and sorrow, release the sorrow and embrace the joy. Feel it. Invite the feeling of joy into every moment of your day. When you are ready, come back to the workbook with your new-found strength.

The way we grow is to notice and be aware of ourselves in experience. If we have changed, we will notice it in our reaction to what used to bother us, what used to hurt us, what used to make us feel belittled etc. We are the creators of our own reality! The first step is to become aware if we have changed over time or are we still reacting the same way we always have? Would you like a different outcome? If so, become aware, stop and choose one.

What My Dreams Say

Dreams give some insight and are important in this journal. If you wish to see, after you have found your mate, if they had any insight for you, then simply keep a journal of them here to reflect, review and see how guided you were in the process. Dreams can come in the form of daydreams, visions and even thoughts out of nowhere that flash across your mind.

Important Notes & Questions

When you clear your mind, in *My Mental Moment*, and do the journaling, you will certainly come up with notes and questions for yourself or others that are not contained in this book. This section is provided for those notes, questions, feelings, desires, etc. that may arise. Jot down any questions that come to you that you would ask your mate or his family. Take note here, of feelings, worries or concerns that surface during this process.

This workbook will help keep you focused. It is suggested to keep it close by for those impromptu thoughts that pop up and use a pencil with a big eraser.

So, grab a pencil, open your heart and mind and let the universe deliver you your perfect mate.

Part One

It's about
YOU

"What is not started today, will never be finished tomorrow."

Johann Wolfgang von Goethe

Get Ready

It is possible and highly likely that ex-boyfriends, husbands or lovers will appear in your life, one way or another, while doing the processes in this book. Why? Often when a relationship is over, we are not ready for it to end. We ponder and wonder why it failed and sometimes go to extremes to bring the ex back into our life. Their arrival during the *Manifest Your Mate* process may be due to an energy stream still flowing from your heart. There may be a hidden string that still connects the two of you. If an ex shows up in your life, while you are trying to manifest a mate, be aware that it could be to test boundaries or to force you to establish them.

Setting boundaries is necessary in all aspects of life and especially when welcoming a new person into your space and heart. Boundaries that allow you to vibrate without fear and/or loss of self in a relationship are great limits to know within yourself. To stick to them, so that you can be the—*you*—that you want to be in a loving relationship. It is your reward.

This manifestation process will test your capability of holding your boundaries in place as your exes arrive, your self-awareness grows and other things you intend appear. Just know this information and be prepared. Any unresolved feelings towards your exes will surface as you do this process. Stick to what you want, all aspects of the person you want to manifest, and you will have the inner power to walk from a relationship that already failed.

You may manifest other things while doing the process. All your thoughts and feelings are causing an energy shift around you. Financial needs may be met. Unexpected travel to unknown places, promotion or better living situations can appear. Your boundaries of belief may be tested as things manifest and shift in your life. The most beneficial aspect of the process is that it reinforces your belief in the power you hold.

A manifestation happened shortly after I finished this manuscript. I had just arrived back from a trip to NY and was driving back from the airport to the house I was staying at. As I was sitting at the red light, about to make a left turn, I thought to myself, *I need to line up a place to stay for a longer period of time, something like 3-8 months.* The next thought was, *I need a place to stay from beginning of October for 3-8 months.* The light changed to green and I continued to the house, unloaded the groceries and settled in to check e-mails.

My phone pinged and alerted me to a text. I read it and my entire body filled with goosebumps. This was about 40 minutes after I was sitting at the light with my thought. This is what I read.

> Hi Joan. Wrote you a couple of emails earlier. I hope you got them. Thanks again for leaving everything in such nice shape. Also, I think I mentioned that we're planning to spend a few months in Dublin later this year. Nothing's set in stone yet, but probably something like beginning or mid-December through the end of March. Wanted to gauge your interest/availability to housesit again.

I had been house sitting for this couple a few weeks earlier. I had received the emails. Dublin hadn't been mentioned in any of them. All that aside, I hadn't spoken to her since I had left her home. This moment solidified in me—thought creates reality. There is nothing else to do but be in sync with your intent and send it out to the Universe. This co-creation action adds your energy to the spin of the Universe and what gets spit out is your manifestation.

December through March was taken care of. I still needed October through November. Two days later I received this text.

> Hi. So, it's looking like we might possibly need to head for Dublin a bit earlier than I thought - perhaps October or mid-September at the very earliest. Nothing set in stone yet, but what does your availability look like for autumn at the moment?

The smile that crept across my face at that moment has not been removed. I knew from experience that I am a co-creator in my life. Each time validation happens, my faith becomes stronger. I hope that you allow your belief system to open to all possibilities. Try not to guide the outcome too much and sit back and see how the Universe delivers. It is quite beautiful.

One never knows if lessons are presented to them or in what format. I share another story with you about manifestation. I had completed the rough draft of this book in July and had a girlfriend quickly check for blatant errors. While she was doing that, she mentioned that someone was coming over tomorrow to use the tennis court and he would arrive at 9 a.m. This was at the house I was sitting in July. As she left she turned and said, "And he is really cute!"

With that news, I decided to wake up early and pull myself together to meet him. After all I was writing a book on manifesting a mate. He practiced tennis alone with the automatic ball machine and kept coming over to speak to me about one thing or another. The hour passed and he asked if I would be there the next day. I said yes. He left.

Later that day, the same girlfriend and I returned some chairs to a neighbor that had been lent for a party I had. This is the same neighbor that organized the *cute guy* to play tennis on the court. As we arrived with the chairs, he said to me, "Michael really liked you."

"Well, I really liked him too. Tell him he can come earlier tomorrow or stay later if he wants." I suddenly spurted out with a smile on my face.

The giddiness that came over me and my girlfriend must have been funny to see. We discussed the fact that the Universe could have manifested a mate that fast, as we hopped up and down like seven-year-old kids.

The next day he arrived and barely said a word, complained about everything when he did speak and vanished quickly. I watched all this happen as I made notes of my experience of manifesting him, for this chapter. My thoughts raced to:

1. *The neighbor instigated my interest by telling me something that I do not know is true.*
2. *Now that he knows I am interested, he is not.*
3. *I must learn the flirting signals all over again.*
4. *How could I jump to such conclusions so fast? Why did I?*

Anyway, the entire episode had to happen at the time it did to show me that I do need to pay attention to flirting signals because if I miss them I am giving off the wrong impression. Also, flirting is part of the mating experience and allows room for the guy to make the next step.

Get Ready

This is just a tip for you as you start on the path. Pay attention. Be aware of the signals of mating.

You meet someone and your heart flutters. The feeling is strange because it has been so long since you felt a stirring in yourself. Your heart is opening and allowing the experience to love again. This guy might not be—the one. That's okay. He is a reminder that you are still a woman. Still desirable and worthy. It's okay to let him down gently. Thank him for the excitement you have about falling in love again. That's why he came into your life. We are all angels for someone.

"If you want it and expect it, it will be yours very soon."

Esther Hicks

Create Space

In the beginning, there is nothing! Plenty of room to create exactly what you want! An artist starts with a blank canvas. A writer with blank paper. A chef starts with an empty pan. From nothing comes something. Creativity flows and happens when you remove obstacles. Preconceived notions, prior emotions and feelings around relationships or men, self-imposed rules or patterns, are several obstacles that block the flow of your own creativity when it comes to the Law of Attraction.

We all have moments in our lives that have preceded this one. These instances are a mixed reality of emotions, feelings, incidents, reactions events, people, places, thoughts and traits that we have carried with us to this point. These are the threads we think weave the fabric of our being. These are the tools and weapons we have used to cultivate and protect the garden of our soul. The different patterns, styles, colors, shapes and textures of these realities are likened to fashion. Some are like an old soft sweater that you pull out when you need to feel comforted. Others are grey and tattered old pants that you don't fit into anymore. Then there are the vivid and bold accessories that you think go with anything and make you stand out in the crowd. Some are just plain out of style and will never come back, like shoulder pads. Some are useful, like gardening gloves and a versatile hat.

Whatever the fashion, one usually dresses for the occasion. When you know, you are going to paint the walls, you find old paint clothes that are already stained and ready to be tossed. When a black-tie affair arrives, you get out the gowns and glitter. When you find yourself in an argument you get out the army gear and defend and protect against the enemy. Sometimes that is your mate. Hopefully the combat gear is in a locked trunk, way in the back of the attic, and is never even thought of these days.

Cleaning out the closet of your life is necessary to make room for a mate. Staying with the fashion analogy, imagine a large walk-in closet. I'm not talking about the one you use every day. I'm talking about that one where you store—*the stuff*—that you may use one day. The stuff you don't want to part with. The stuff you accepted as a gift and shoved in a drawer long ago. The stuff an ex gave you and you put it away when you broke up. All the things from your childhood that your mom thought you should keep. That is the closet I am speaking of. The closet of your life experiences.

I have moved many times in my life. With each move I've gotten rid of tons of things that collected since the last move. I don't go out and get a lot of stuff but as time goes by these things add up. I do believe that most of us would fill every single inch of our living space or storage space with stuff, if we didn't think others would think poorly of us. Currently I have a storage unit that has things that I decided, upon my last move, I wanted to keep. I am sure when I move it out of there I will only leave with half of it. What I am getting to is that we all think we need things that we will use one day. We store, pay for and lug around for years and then we get rid of them anyway. At one point, we know we can't use it, don't need it, don't want it or it is no longer in fashion.

When your house—*you*—is crammed full of unnecessary things, there is no room for anyone to get in. Past ways of thinking and reacting that you refuse to look at and change, are barriers to your future. So, when Mr. Perfect arrives, you won't have room for him. Those *past* things are cluttering up your space and view. You may not know that he is at the door. Also, he can't see the *real you* through the *old you*.

You were conceived. You began. Since that moment, you have stored things. Some of these things are from the past, not remembered, but control you to this day, on many levels including physical. Some are useful. Some are not. The patterns, textures and hues of these choices may not serve you well in your present life. They may need to be removed from the— *closet*. Identified for what they are and why you got them in the first place. Thank them for being useful till now and then toss them away. Then you can fill the closet with a new image of yourself. An updated version for the current attitudes and responses you would prefer as the adult you are now.

Once the clutter of your emotional life is organized, then when you ask for your mate, you have room to receive him. Ask and you shall receive. It doesn't say, Ask and you will receive! You must be ready, willing and able to receive what you ask for. Open yourself, your heart and your space to receive.

Here is an example of how to make a good Universal Order.

My statement would be: I am open to receive my perfect mate.

A more precise affirmation is a better choice. Ask to get what you want, when you are ready, willing and able.

I intended to start *Manifest Your Mate* on August 1st, along with twelve other women that agreed to be part of a short test group for the book. At that time, I got thrown curve balls left and right. First, a great fashion campaign that took me to New York. Second, the demise of a dear friend of mine eventually took me away from my plans and back to Texas to assist in any way I could. Third, there was a house-sitting gig relinquished due to my friend in Texas.

While back in Texas, another friend reached out for design ideas. I decided to help her with her home before I had to depart to Nevada. Once the walls were opened and wires exposed, my main contractor ended up in the hospital. This threw me into a tizzy of needing to find someone, anyone, to help finish the job before my departure to Nevada. After 4 days, I did. That crunched my time and there was no time for me to start the processes in *Manifest Your Mate*.

I put it aside to handle and complete the design job, knowing I would get back to it the minute I had a moment. That time ended up being in Nevada. As I was traveling via car to Nevada, I realized I had time to work on some powerful and precise affirmations. I was prepping the Universe, for the delivery of my mate.

Being specific in making a statement is the key. Here are my first ones:

- I will meet my mate in Nevada.
- I will meet my mate while staying in Nevada.
- I will meet my mate while living in Nevada.

Those three statements each mean something entirely different.

The first one states that I will meet my mate in Nevada. Okay, maybe I will. However, I am staying there for a few months. So, that does mean that I won't travel outside of Nevada during the time I am staying there? No. So, I could meet my mate while staying in Nevada but not meet him physically in Nevada.

The second statement is more true, because it allows for me to meet my mate while staying in Nevada, no matter where or when I stay there. However, it broadens the time span. So, a better statement would be, if I wish to meet him sooner than later:

- I will meet my mate while I am staying in Nevada from October through December.

That shortens my time of meeting my mate within those three months and gives a delivery deadline.

The third states, *living,* which means something different, than *staying*.

The perfect statement for me would be:
- I will meet my mate while staying in Nevada during the period of October 2016 through December 2016.

This allows me to meet him anywhere in the world in that period and that I will meet him then.

The above statement does not mean that we will hook up, marry, move in etc. It simply means that we will meet. Notice, I did not mention facts of "how" it would happen.

The more specific you are in the announcement to the Universe the more precise your request will be met.

Practice writing a precise affirmation here that will guide you in your endeavor:

_____

_____

_____

_____

_____

_____

_____

_____

_____

_____

_____

_____

_____

_____

_____

_____

_____

_____

_____

"Sometimes I wonder if men and women really suit each other. Perhaps they should live next door and just visit now and then."

Katherine Hepburn

Let's Get Real

You are the accumulation of all that has come before you that is directly related to you. That's a lot of energy, a lot of traits, just a lot to carry around! Most of it you are not even aware of because these traits show up in the way you react to things, people, places, foods etc. You don't know why. It just is. You can't remember why from your early years. You certainly can't remember any of the stuff your parents have hidden in their closets or hope chests.

So, to commence bringing in the perfect mate for you, it is necessary to walk into that hidden closet where all these *things* are kept. Take a good look at your collector's items. Hold them up and look at them in your new light. Experience and enjoy your new point of view. Now touch them. Feel if you need them to go forward. Dust them off. Look at them for what they really are. Are they beneficial to your needs now? Are they keeping you from getting what you want?

They are either traits that you really *need* to move forward in your life, the way you want, or things you *don't need* that will only get in your way to happiness and bliss.

This is the first step to bringing in your mate. One that will vibe with you at a deeper level. One that will have the perfect chance of staying power and longevity. One that will be your rock, no matter what. You are the first step.

That first step is revamping the *you* that you have become is to create space for your new mate. A space that is nurturing, whole, loving and understanding. A new attitude will attract a mate that has gone through his own closet and has space for you and your stuff in it.

If a relationship is a mirror, it means it reflects those traits that we need to deal with. Then we need to look at our relationships: relationships with our parents, friends, loves, marriages, work etc. This first chapter is the most in-depth because we must clean out our own house—*self*—before we can have a true relationship that is capable of withstanding time. After all, if the mirror analogy is correct, wouldn't it be better to have fewer negative things to deal with in the next relationship?

Circle five words from the list below that you would describe yourself as:

Angry	Intelligent	Adventurous
Caring	Picky	Honest
Open	Weak	Patient
Unlovable	Complex	Silent
Flawed	Selfish	Safe
Crazy	Faithful	Poised
Simple	Sick	Loud
Lost	Kind	Unpredictable
Sexy	Grateful	Exceptional
Studious	Cruel	Smart
Solid	Close-Minded	Cool
Hurtful	Courageous	Soft
Disturbed	Hopeful	Childlike
Introverted	Perfectionist	Funny

Are you aware of any traits that you dislike in yourself?

This is the place you put those things that you know get in your way. Putting them here will allow you to look at them, notice them, bring focus to them and eventually thank them. Forgive yourself and get rid of or alter these, so that you can wear them better and more fashionably in your future.

_____

_____

_____

_____

_____

_____

_____

_____

_____

_____

_____

_____

_____

_____

_____

_____

For instance, here's one of mine that I am working on.

In conversation, I listen, but will have an idea or thought that I know I will lose if I don't interject at that moment, so I interject. Do you like it when someone does that to you? I don't. Over time I have become aware of that trait and I try my hardest not to interject. I try to wait for the proper moment to say my thought. Lots of times, by the time I get the chance to interject, I have forgotten what I was going to say. So, was it that important to begin with? No! It's probably a habit I picked up by watching others at a young age converse. That is how my parents probably did it. So, that is what I have done most of my life.

Have you been told by anyone you love; maybe a spouse, ex, parent and/or a good friend, that there are some things, or one specific, in your personality that you could soften or exchange?

If so, place these here. List the person who made you aware of them. When you are ready to take a hard look inside at how these have forged your life, relationships and friendships, you can come to this page and thank the person who brought this to your attention. If you choose, call them up and tell them how they have helped you make some changes for the better and that you appreciate their honesty and guidance.

_____

_____

_____

_____

_____

_____

_____

_____

_____

_____

_____

_____

Here's one of mine.

A good friend, who will remain nameless, told me one time that I need to stop being so intense. I asked what they meant. They said, "You get going on a subject and never stop." *Yeah, so?* I thought at the time. They told me that most of the time they have no interest or understanding about what I am saying and just sit politely waiting for me to finish.

I asked myself, *is this my issue or theirs?* Why didn't they just tell me to shut up? I thought about it for a moment. I am passionate and when I am passionate about something I must show it by bringing up endless facts with people I feel comfortable with.

My friend was mentioning this to me because she feels it hinders me from meeting my next mate. It was a dating tip. I have taken it to heart and now try to limit the amount of time I speak about a topic. If they ask me about something I might just preface my response with, "I get passionate about some things and have a habit of rambling on with intensity. Please stop me when you are on overload." I am still practicing.

What are your fears?

List what you know you are afraid of and any phobias. Fear is the opposite of love and cannot exist at the same time as love. Fear is: *Fictitious Events Appearing Real.* Most of us fear things and we have no idea why. For instance, the fear of snakes, if you have never encountered one. The fear of heights with never falling from a tall building. Why are these things in us?

These are experiences that our relatives had and that energy is still going strong. If it is not dealt with it gets passed along, like the bread basket at dinner, until you take the last piece and state: *There is no more bread (fear).* You may come back to this page and deal with these fears however you choose. We are programmed to believe that life should be difficult. We are taught that we must work hard to achieve our desires. A new thought is—life should be joyous and it is easy to overcome anything.

_____

_____

_____

_____

_____

_____

_____

_____

_____

_____

_____

_____

Here is one of mine:

I don't think I would want someone to hold my head under water or suffocate me to death. I don't know if that is a fear or a survival trait, but it wouldn't be pleasant. I was claustrophobic and had no idea why. Nothing had happened in my life that I remembered that would have caused that. In my modeling days, I would arrive early to set so that I could make sure that I did not get any turtlenecks. Just putting on a turtleneck caused me to panic. I got over that and I have plenty of turtlenecks now. I don't have many fears, however. When I think of the future, I fill it with good stuff. Hey, if we can fill it with anything we wish, why would I fill it with *fear*.

What is holding you back in any area of your life?

List here any known obstacles that you believe are hindering your growth, happiness, finances, health etc. This may take another sheet of paper. Being aware if you blame others for your shortcomings would also be something to list here. Some of us just accept how things are and deal with it. Some of us rebel against change. Some of us take action and steps to change what we believe are roadblocks to our success in anything. When you can clearly see your obstacles, then you can take the proper steps to make change, or not. The clearer your path is in front of you, the easier it will be for your mate to run on it towards you.

_____

_____

_____

_____

_____

_____

_____

_____

_____

_____

_____

_____

_____

_____

_____

_____

_____

_____

_____

_____

_____

_____

_____

_____

_____

_____

_____

_____

_____

Here is one of mine.

I recently took a long hard look at my life now. A discovery was made. I have never stopped going full speed ahead since I left Texas to go to Paris to model in 1977. This year I finally took a step back and looked at what I want in my life for the future.

Now I am making stronger decisions. Career, location, relationship changes and some core belief shifts have redirected my life. Away from where it was going and into the wild blue yonder! Plans have been thrown out the window and I am learning to go with my gut instincts instead of my thinker. I am learning to feel and sense again, after years of just running in the rat race. Amazement is all I can say as each day brings clarity in one direction or another. This clarity guides my choices in which bonds to severe and which to keep glued together in my life.

Have you lost anyone dear to you?

List here, anyone, including pets, who has passed on. Next to their name note what responsibility you feel in their passing. List anything you wished you could have said to them, any feelings that you still hold toward them. This will be a place to come back and reflect upon from time to time in your life. Pull the strengths from those who gave them to you. Let go of the negative emotions and feelings toward those who have passed. Thank them for your experience together, whether good or bad and forgive yourself in your reactions. We are all children dealing and coping with hidden stuff in our toy box.

_____

_____

_____

_____

_____

_____

_____

_____

Here is one of mine:

My dog. This was the hardest thing in my life that I have had to deal with. She became ill after 14 years of life. Each time I took her to the vet, they stuck drainage tubes in her. They drained the liquid out of her so she could last another month. This went on for several months when I asked, "What is the point, Doc? Will she ever get better or will this have to happen forever?"

He said. "We can probably keep her alive for a few more months. That's just prolonging the inevitable."

I knew I would have to put her down.

Recently a psychic spurted out in a class of about thirty. "Who yelled at their dog?" and he pointed at me as he said it.

I looked puzzled in his direction and silently inferred "Me???"
I tried to defend myself against that remark and then I sat and thought. Did *I yell at my dog?*

I probably screamed at her a few times when she ate my leather shoes. Or that time I screamed at her to *stop* so she would not get hit by a car. Then I became silent inside and out. I sat with the thought that her spirit is still around. I realized *I can connect with her at any time.*

My heart reopened a bit as tears ran down my cheeks and slipped into my mouth. It was a quenching thought that will stay with me forever. I knew that her spirit held that scolding/warning as a pain. She obviously came through in that psychic setting to let me know that I can still heal the situation and by healing it with forgiveness I can move forward, remove my guilt and release her from any misunderstanding she must have had at that time as well.

"No matter how good a woman you are, you will never be good enough to a man that isn't ready"

Unknown

Finding Your Inner Mate

The test group results revealed that many women stopped the processes in this book because they realized they had inner work to do. They thought they couldn't or didn't want to, manifest a mate until they had "fixed" their issues.

This is wonderful information. We must heal our own house before it is a place someone would want to visit, but remodeling can happen forever. There will always be something that you want to change or work on. Life is about change and becoming aware. It is a lifelong process.

Why wait until you have fixed everything you think you need to change about yourself to seek a mate? You could be well over one hundred years old by the time that perfection occurs. In certain belief systems, perfection can only occur when you become one with the One again.

So, when the feelings arise, that you can't have a mate in your life now because you have so much work to do on yourself, think about it this way instead:

We all evolve, including your mate. Bringing someone into your life that can grow with you, accept your changes and change with you over time would be a wonderful mate to have. Make that part of your manifestation.

Why waste the prime of your life?

Growth happens. Change happens. Everything is in constant flux. Relationships change over time. The ups and downs on the ladder of love happen to us to make us grow. The more experiences we have, the happier the Universe is. We are here to create everything! It doesn't have to be done solo. It's okay if it is, but having someone on the other side of the ladder can make life's journey more exciting. Especially when you have worked so hard to develop your side of the ladder.

Imaging a ladder being made. There are two solid sides. You are one side and the mate you seek is the other. This ladder is made of wood and the two sides are growing trees in a forest of life. Your density, flexibility, age and type are perfect to build the ladder to love. You chose each other to create this ladder.

You stand afar from each other, with certain rungs of qualities that shine, strong and weak. You stand side by side but worlds apart until, like two strong trees in a forest with branches outstretched, you touch and intermingle.

The ladder to a loving relationship starts with both persons being whole. Is one ever truly whole in the human form? We always strive, grow, want, need, aspire to be or have more. If we wait until we are *perfect,* we will miss out on sharing the experience with someone. That someone is seeking their mate as well.

Each rail stands securely on its footing. The rungs; qualities, feelings, emotions, desires and wishes reach from the sides, like arms, towards each other. Some are longer than the others and some are shorter. Some extend clear over to the others and are ready to embrace it as part of its own. Some need nurturing and assurance along the way. Some just need to know there is another rung feeling the same way.

As these rungs meet and adjoin, a strong base is created. Once established, tested and trusted, your couple can use it to extend as far as you wish. Together you grow into your future knowing that the ladder of love will not topple or crumble under the weight of life's events.

In this analogy, you can see why it is important to develop a strong foundation before expecting anything to unfold as you wish it to.

The concepts presented in this journal will provide a clear and fast track to your desires. This is a practice. The more you use these principles and focus your intent, in all areas of your life, the quicker your ability to manifest becomes. Then, one day you will have a thought fulfilled within seconds of you thinking it. If you are aware at that moment, you might be stunned at the reality you just created. After the truth sets in, you will understand. You are the co-creator of your life, your relationships and everything you can possibly imagine. Enjoy the process!

Part Two

It's about HIM

"The muscular athletic type is not representative of the human race, who are varied in their physique."

Vivienne Westwood

Let's Get Physical

Although most of us will never admit it, the physical aspect of a person is very important and usually the first thing we attract to, when we meet someone. After all, the physical is the first thing we see. And sight is one of our first senses used in almost everything we do. We have preset biological information in our brains that cause us to react when we see a lion coming toward us. These programs have helped us survive until this day as species. So, when it comes to finding a mate, physical chemistry is important.

It is stated that most men and women look for their *Mother or Father* when seeking a mate. This makes sense. We are programmed that this is the best way for us to survive, because our parent/parents provided our food and shelter. It was coded into our biological information. So, we seek the physical as well as any other traits to fill those shoes, even if the traits are not nurturing or loving.

I discovered this after joining a matchmaking service. I voluntarily filled out a form that assisted the service in finding me my perfect match. I answered questions ranging from "How much money does he need to make?" to "Does he want children?". I then offered up my own criteria costume for my mate to fit into. I closed my list of desires with, *after all that, if there is no attraction (chemistry) the above criteria need not be met.*

After several matches through this service, I realized I had not been specific enough in the physical attributes of the type of person that I find attractive. The matches had been too short, too old, too plain, too whatever. I was not attracted to any of them. These were physical things. I couldn't believe I was so shallow! But I was. That is why this section is important and first in the book. You may wish to skip to another chapter and start there first. There is no specified order, as we are all different.

What is the first thing you notice when a member of the opposite sex approaches you, to ask a question or engage you in conversation? Is it their height, weight, smile, eyes, attire, hair, skin color or ethnicity? Is it their breath, cologne or voice? Is it the size of their hands or feet?

The first thing we notice is usually a physical trait. We are attracted to them, because of a physical trait. We determine if we will: have a conversation, accept an invitation to meet elsewhere, exchange numbers or jump in the sack right away, on a physical level. So, we are all shallow when it comes to this and it is a good thing, as sometimes it takes the physical attraction to get to the next step. Many men, on their online dating profiles, state they prefer a woman who is in good physical shape. Why? Because they are innately attracted, by biological programs, to seek someone who is capable to procreate. And these programs run the show. If a female is in good shape, she can carry a pregnancy to term and raise the child. This ensures that the genetics of the man survive. It's all about survival on certain levels.

If you have ever seen pigeons trying to mate you will notice that the female avoids, ignores and removes herself from a male that she deems not fit to mate with. Animals have criteria which is innate when it comes to mating. The fittest survive in the animal kingdom. It is all quite biological!

The statement regarding race has few choices, as scientifically humanity has only three races, at time of publication.

- Caucasian races (Aryans, Hamites, Semites)
- Mongolian races (northern Mongolian, Chinese and Indo-Chinese, Japanese and Korean, Tibetan, Malayan, Polynesian, Māori, Micronesian, Eskimo, American Indian),
- Negroid races (African, Hottentots, Melanesians/Papua, "Negrito," Australian Aborigine, Dravidians, Sinhalese)

After filling in the physical attributes of your soon-to-be delivered mate you will have narrowed the search down a bit, but not by much. It will be necessary to continue with the internal traits they possess, their profession, demeanor, family life, wants and needs, etc.

Take a Mental Moment and go ahead and start molding the physical person you want to appear in your life.

His Physical Attributes

My mate is between:

_____ ft./m _____ in /cm   and   _____ ft./m _____ in /cm

My mate is:

_____ lbs. / kilos   or between   _____ & _____ lbs. / kilos

My mate's skin color is:

lighter than darker   darker, than lighter   white
black   olive
Other_____

_____

My mate's build is:

thin   thick   heavy   overweight   fit
round   big-boned   muscular
Other_____

_____

My mate's face is:

oval   rectangular   square   round   thin   chiseled
triangular
Other_____

_____

My mate's complexion is:

flawless   weathered   ageless   scarred   freckled
youthful

Let's Get Physical

Other_____
_____

My mate's hair color is:

   brown   black   blonde   red   grey   S&P
   dyed   fake
   Other_____
   _____

My mate's hair is:

   thick   thin   curly   wavy   straight   a wig
   non-existent   a toupee   plugs   extensions

   Other_____
   _____

My mate's eyes are:

   blue   brown   black   green   hazel   glass
   missing
   Other_____
   _____
   _____

My mate's eyes are:

   round   almond   small   large   square   cat-
   like   intense
   Other_____
   _____

Manifest Your Mate

My mate's vision is:

perfect   contacts   glasses   bifocals   blind
laser-like
Other_____

_____

My mate's lips are:

thin   full   pouty   big   baby-like   turned-up
turned-down   always smiling   injected
sweet   soft   sexy
Other_____

_____

My mate's shoe size is:

Size _____   Width _____
Other_____

_____

My mate's feet are:

small for their height soft calloused average big
for their height
Other_____

_____

My mate's toes are:

squared across the top   long   pointed   short
buffed rounded across the top   cute   stubby
always polished
Other_____

_____

Let's Get Physical

My mate's hands are:

soft   calloused   average   squared   big
small   tender
Other_____

_____

My mate's fingers are:

pointy   rounded   square   gnarled   long
short   stubby
Other_____

_____

My mate's finger nails are:

buffed   clean   dirty   bitten   hard   soft
manicured
Other_____

_____

My mate's race is:

Negroid   Mongolian   Caucasian   ET

My mate's lineage is:

European   Chinese   African   Australian   Japanese
Russian   N. American   Indian   Nat. Am.
Mid. Eastern   Scandinavian   South American
Eastern Block   United Kingdom
Other_____

_____

Manifest Your Mate

Take a moment. Take a breath and close your eyes. Imagine the first time you see your mate. Let this imaginary moment start to create a feeling. How do you feel? What emotions are running through you? What are your first thoughts? When you have that moment well engraved on your mind, write it down on the next few lines.

_____

_____

_____

_____

_____

_____

_____

_____

_____

_____

_____

_____

If you wish, make a list of some famous people, people you know or renowned people that your mate will have qualities of below.

My mate will have:

eyes like _____lips like _____

hair like _____ a body like _____

will look like

_____

is tall like

_____

a smile like

_____

Meaningful Memories or Triggers

_____

_____

_____

_____

_____

_____

_____

_____

_____

_____

_____

_____

_____

_____

_____

What My Dreams Say

Use these pages to follow your dreams while creating your mate. Dreams are very powerful connections into your deepest self and the universe. You may be surprised by the information you collect on your soon to be delivered mate.

_____

_____

_____

_____

_____

_____

_____

_____

_____

_____

_____

_____

_____

_____

_____

_____

_____

_____

_____

_____

Let's Get Physical

Manifest Your Mate

Important Notes & Questions

You may think of some questions that are not in this book. Keeping track of them when you think of them will benefit you in creating your mate.

_____

_____

_____

_____

_____

_____

_____

_____

_____

_____

_____

_____

_____

_____

_____

_____

_____

_____

_____

_____

Let's Get Physical

"When he spoke, what tender words he used! So softly, that like flakes of feathered snow, they melted as they fell."

John Dryden

Who Are they?

Now that the Universe is aware of some physical traits of your potential mate, you will have hundreds of opportunities coming your way, maybe even thousands. They may all be very close to your actual physical description of your mate, but there will be far too many choices and too little time. This section is where you can get deeper into who this person is. It will help you free up some time by not wasting as much energy on the wrong person. After all, you will be busy deciding who to speak with or go out with, now that choices are being delivered to you.

What type of personality do they have? Are they basically happy by nature? What sends them into depression? These sorts of questions are important to know about someone because you can decide if you will be compatible, based upon these realities. Do you want someone who needs your constant attention? What level of nurturing do they need, on a daily basis? It takes years to see all the personality traits in someone. *Manifest Your Mate* will shorten that time frame. You will already know who they are because you created them. Your intention invited them to your door.

Is your mate a Type A personality? Is he shy? Is he a clown in public? Is he a child at heart? What are the personality traits that are most noticeable in your mate? During your discovery process, you will be pleasantly surprised at how many of your requirements they may meet. Falling in love is just a short step away.

Take a Mental Moment and go ahead and give him a personality!

Who Are They?

His Personality Traits

My mate is generally:

happy   lethargic   hyper   content   quiet
depressed   calm
Other_____

_____

My mate is:

very sociable   uncomfortable in crowds   shy
introverted   extroverted   over the top
wild   a real comedian
Other_____

_____

My mate communicates with me best:

by phone   e-mail   letters   face to face
sign language   by not saying a word
with music   greeting cards
Other_____

_____

When my mate is angry they:

leave the room to cool down   scream and yell
get rough   get sarcastic   get even
get another mate   go to the gym
Other_____

_____

Manifest Your Mate

My mate is:

very funny   never laughs at anything   relevant
is the life of the party   poignant
listens but rarely joins in
Other_____

_____

When my mate is nervous he:

sweats   laughs   cries   leaves the room   gets
quiet   gets loud   makes jokes   drinks or smokes
copes with it
Other_____

_____

At a dinner party, my mate is:

polite   too polite   rude   proper
clueless   intense always the center of attention
prefers I do all the talking
Other_____

_____

When we are dating my mate always:

opens my car door   pulls out my chair
pours my water/wine   asks what I want to eat
brings me flowers or a gift   is prompt
makes the reservations   finds the venues
is complimentary
Other_____

_____

Who Are They?

When coming to my house for dinner my mate:

      usually cooks it too   brings dinner
      brings a friend   offers to bring something
      brings flowers   helps in the kitchen
      watches T.V. until it's done   suggests take out
      is never hungry
      Other_____

      _____

My mate:

      leaves wet towels on furniture   cleans up after himself
      air dries   never bathes   has servants
      uses a bath robe
      Other_____

      _____

My mate:
      has children   wants children   is a child   has a pet
      lost a child   needs nurturing   loves children
      doesn't want any children
      Other_____

      _____

My mate would say that they are/have/do:

      doing the best, they can   ready to practice all
      they have learned   know it all   been
      there/done that   wants me to teach him
      Other_____

      _____

Manifest Your Mate

When it comes to astrology my mate:

can't spell it   can't leave home without it
reads the horoscope sometimes
does not believe in it   writes the horoscope
Other_____

_____

My mate makes decisions:

easily   quickly   too quickly   is wishy washy
cannot make a decision   always takes charge
with integrity
Other_____

_____

My mate is:

a worrywart   pensive   intense   argumentative
intellectual   obsessive   passionate
politically correct   sensitive
Other_____

_____

When my mate is alone he:

studies   calls me often   meditates   does yoga
reads   writes   spends time with his pets
watches sports
Other_____

_____

Take a Mental Moment. Take a breath and become the space that is your consciousness. Imagine discovering your mate's personality traits for the first time. What is most noticeable? What is a hidden undertone? What makes you smile? How do you feel? How does he bring out the joy in you?

_____

_____

_____

_____

_____

_____

_____

_____

_____

_____

Meaningful Memories or Triggers

_____

_____

_____

_____

_____

_____

_____

What My Dreams Say

Use these pages to follow your dreams while creating your mate. Dreams are very powerful connections into your deepest self and the universe. You may be surprised by the information you collect on your soon to be delivered mate.

_____

_____

_____

_____

_____

_____

_____

_____

_____

_____

_____

_____

_____

_____

_____

_____

_____

_____

_____

_____

_____

_____

_____

Who Are They?

Important Notes & Questions

You may think of some questions that are not in this book. Keeping track of them when you think of them will benefit you in creating your mate.

_____
_____
_____
_____
_____
_____
_____
_____
_____
_____
_____
_____
_____
_____
_____
_____
_____
_____
_____

Who Are They?

"Most doctors are prisoners of their education and shackled by their profession."

Richard Diaz

Profession

Although it shouldn't matter what your mate does for a living, sometimes we click with people in certain professions. You may like someone who loves to talk about your interests more than theirs. Others may want someone they learn things from. Someone more knowledgeable than themselves. Maybe you are looking for someone to take care of you financially. Or someone retired, so you can travel the world together.

Your mate's profession determines a lot of things about your relationship. Where you will live may depend on where he works. When you have children, will he be able to take off work to help you out? Does his job offer medical coverage for his soon-to-be spouse?

Questions like these are very important when reality sets in. Let's say you have met the mate of your dreams. Everything has gone smoothly up till now. Now there is a glitch! They have a better paying job than you and they live on the opposite coast. Your family, friends and job are not where his job is. How willing are you to uproot yourself and be perfectly happy with your decision?

Do child custody terms, allow you to relocate? Will your children want to leave their friends? Will your new mate uproot himself? Do you toss a coin to see? Will your family disown you if you move away? Will you be homesick? Will he? Will finances permit travel at Thanksgiving or other holidays?

Some professions call for twenty-four hour stand by, while others are nine to five. Some artistic professions involve traveling all over the world. Some have you locked in an editing bay for weeks on end. Some are stressful, like being a doctor. Some are dangerous, like working on an offshore oil rig. It might not matter to you what your mate does as long as he brings home the paycheck. Or you could be one that worries if he will be coming home at all, like a policeman or soldier.

Take a Mental Moment to make space for the profession of your mate to become clear and give him a job, one that will vibe with a lifestyle you desire.

His Profession

My mate is a:

      lawyer   doctor   politician   teacher   salesperson
      manager   student   unemployed   pro athlete
      singer   actor   retired
      Other_____

_____

My mate's salary is:

      _____   per year   per month   a day an hour
      non-existent   sporadic   trust fund   borrowed
      Other_____

_____

My mate's job, offers:

      spousal coverage   paid vacation   business
      travel   long hours   a bonus   baby-leave
      expenses paid   mileage   status
      Other_____

_____

My mate's work day is:

      _____ hrs. a day

My mate works:

      4 day weeks   5 day weeks   6 day weeks
      7 day weeks 8 day weeks   as little as possible
      because he wants to

Other_____

_____

My mate enjoys:

having lunch at the office   meeting me for lunch
doesn't eat lunch   having business lunches
working out at lunchtime
Other_____

_____

When it comes to his job, my mate is:

professional   punctual   lazy   tardy
enthusiastic   going through the motions   careless
interested   the boss   trying to save the world
waiting for a better offer
Other_____

_____

My mate has had this job for:

_____ months   years   days   hours   minutes
Other_____

_____

My mate:

brings work home   leaves the job at the office

can't wait to   get home   thinks about his job

while at home   works at home   is married to his

job   is in the family biz   wants to win the lottery

Other_____

_____

Profession

My mate wishes to:

remain where he is at his job   get a raise

resign   quit   be a Mr. mom

go into business with me

Other_____

_____

My mate has had previous jobs as a:

mechanic   plumber   server   retail sales

assistant   cook   handyman   accountant

pilot   teacher   trader   CEO

Other_____

_____

Take a Mental Moment. Take a breath. Close your eyes and imagine your physical mate with his best personality traits when you see him at his profession for the first time. How do you feel when you see the whole package doing his thing? What are your first thoughts?

_____

_____

_____

_____

_____

_____

_____

_____

_____
_____
_____
_____
_____
_____
_____
_____
_____

Meaningful Memories or Triggers

_____
_____
_____
_____
_____
_____
_____
_____
_____
_____
_____
_____
_____
_____
_____
_____
_____

What My Dreams Say

Use these pages to follow your dreams while creating your mate. Dreams are very powerful connections into your deepest self and the universe. You may be surprised by the information you collect on your soon to be delivered mate.

_____

_____

_____

_____

_____

_____

_____

_____

_____

_____

_____

_____

_____

_____

_____

_____

_____

_____

_____

_____

_____

Manifest Your Mate

Important Notes & Questions

You may think of some questions that are not in this book. Keeping track of them when you think of them will benefit you in creating your mate.

_____

_____

_____

_____

_____

_____

_____

_____

_____

_____

_____

_____

_____

_____

_____

_____

_____

_____

_____

_____

_____

_____

_____

_____

_____

_____

_____

_____

_____

_____

_____

_____

_____

_____

_____

_____

_____

_____

_____

_____

_____

_____

_____

_____

_____

_____

_____

_____

_____

_____

_____

"Women may be able to fake orgasms, but men can fake whole relationships."

James Shubert

Track Record

When looking for a mate, the relationship they have with parents, siblings, ex-wives and even substance abuse, counts big time. Especially how those relationships exist now. The types of relationships they have had in the past with lovers, spouses, drugs and most of all parents and siblings, should be important to you. You may decide to change some things along your path but you should never think that you will change his. That's up to him.

Were his prior relationships short, medium or long? Is he the commitment type or does he go along until he gets kicked out or forced into a marriage proposal? What was his last relationship based on? Where did he want it to go? I know living in the moment is a thing men do better than women, but in a relationship, especially with marriage and children on your mind, thinking for the future, is a good quality to look for.

Do you want children? Does he want children? Does he have children? Does he have grandchildren? How will his children be affected when you become part of their lives? Will your kids get along with his kids? Does he still support them? Are his kids grown adults?

If he had communication problems with his previous partners, has he resolved the patterns that created the problems? If there was vast conflict in his past relationship/s, was he in it because he liked the battle or needed it? The answers to these questions will be a huge barometer for you and the decisions you make. If his mother can do no wrong, then you will have to become her for the relationship to work. If your daddy always put his little girl on a pedestal, make sure you have the perfect place to set it and show your new guy where it is.

When someone goes out to buy a house, they do not buy it solely based on what they see on the outside. That is the first impression, it gets them in the door. What makes them want to know more about the house? When they enter and they see things they like. The kitchen is great, the bedrooms are perfect, there are no leaks in the roof, the slab is not cracked. The windows are clear and do not rattle at the slightest breeze. All the above are parts of a person also.

Does your mate have a good head on his shoulders? Does he rattle when things get tough? Is he cracked from a previous experience and has he had *foundation* repair? Do you have a solid foundation? Does he have a big heart? Is he comfortable in the bedroom? Is he addicted to a substance? Is he medicated on prescription drugs?

These are the important things about your mate. After these discoveries, if you decide to go further, have the inspector—best friend—come in before you invest your time. The following questions will help you create a mate that will meet your criteria and solidify a good deal so that foreclosure is not in your future.

Take a Mental Moment and see how your mate's past has improved him and made him the man who is right for you. Everyone has a past. It's how it is pasted into the now, that determines how your mate will stick to your life.

His Track Record

My mate had their first serious romantic relationship when they were:

     a toddler   a teen   20 something   30 something

     40 something   over 50   ours is his first

     Other_____

_____

The above-mentioned relationship lasted (how many):

     _____ years   months   days   hours   minutes

In this relationship:

     they didn't have intercourse   they had intercourse

     kissing and fondling only   lots of porn flicks

     cunnilingus

     Other_____

_____

My mate was this age the first time they had sexual intercourse:

     under 16   between 16 & 18   between 18-21

     between 21-35   they are still waiting for me

     Other_____

_____

Manifest Your Mate

My mate has been to therapy:

since a child   after his first relationship   he can't
spell the word   during his first marriage
his mother is his therapist   therapy isn't for him
thinks it is for women only
Other_____

_____

My mate thinks conversation is:

for sports announcers   something Oprah does well
revealing   not necessary   for women only
a good joke   silence   a way to please me
stimulating   therapeutic   necessary
Other_____

_____

An argument with my mate happens when I say:

What do you want for dinner?   Is this pink or purple?
I disagree.   My mate never argues   Good Morning
I'm having girlfriends over.
My mother is coming for the weekend.
Where have you been?
Other_____

_____

My mate forgives me by:

letting me have my way   gifting me   hugging me
waiting 3 days to have sex   telling me so

patting my shoulder   never forgives me
Other_____

My mate's previous experience with children was:

volunteering at the zoo   babysat when they were 12
in their dreams   their sibling has children
kicking them off the basketball court last week
they were a child once

Other_____

My mate:

never owned their own place   still lives at home
rents a home   has a roommate   is homeless
            has more than one roommate
lives in an apartment   lives in their own home
Other_____

When it comes to parking tickets, my mate:

has never had one   rips them up   always pays
them   walks now   can't find the last one
has a warrant for his arrest   has a bike
Other_____

Manifest Your Mate

When it comes to court, my mate:

       was never in one   divorce court only   is a lawyer
       was a judge   awaits trial   is allergic   is a judge
       was a juror   is a bailiff
       Other_____

_____

My mate loves to hang out with his friends:

       at their place   at my place   at a bar   at a strip
       club   at the spa   at a cigar bar   at the mall
       at the gym   at a restaurant
       Other_____

_____

My mate's relationship with their mother is:

       aggressive   non-existent   loving   smothering
       too close   wonderful   she's deceased
       she wants grandchildren   estranged
       Other_____

_____

My mate ended his last relationship/marriage by:

       cheating   he didn't end it, she did   he's still married
       taking all the stuff & filing for divorce   a phone call
       a text
       Other_____

_____

Track Record

My mate's relationship with his father is:

estranged   he is like a brother   he's deceased
still competitive   combative   passive
loving   genuine   caring for him
Other_____

_____

If my mate has kids (under 18) he has custody:

every other day   every other week   every
other weekend   solely   he has visiting rights
he has no right to see his kids
Other_____

_____

Take a Mental Moment. Take a breath. Close your eyes and imagine your mate in different situations as mentioned above and see his responses. Note which ones make you feel filled with joy and love. Which ones make you laugh or cry?

_____
_____
_____
_____
_____
_____
_____

_____

_____

_____

_____

_____

_____

_____

_____

_____

_____

Meaningful Memories or Triggers

_____

_____

_____

_____

_____

_____

_____

_____

_____

_____

_____

Track Record

What My Dreams Say

Use these pages to follow your dreams while creating your mate. Dreams are very powerful connections into your deepest self and the universe. You may be surprised by the information you collect on your soon to be delivered mate.

_____

_____

_____

_____

_____

_____

_____

_____

_____

_____

_____

_____

_____

_____

_____

_____

_____

_____

_____

_____

_____

Manifest Your Mate

_____

_____

_____

_____

_____

_____

_____

_____

_____

_____

_____

_____

_____

_____

_____

_____

_____

_____

_____

_____

_____

_____

_____

_____

_____

_____

_____

_____

Important Notes & Questions

You may think of some questions that are not in this book. Keeping track of them when you think of them will benefit you in creating your mate.

_____

_____

_____

_____

_____

_____

_____

_____

_____

_____

_____

_____

_____

_____

_____

_____

_____

_____

_____

_____

Manifest Your Mate

"A kiss is a lovely trick designed by nature to stop speech when words become superfluous."

Ingrid Bergman

SEX-perience Counts

Does size matter? Well if it matters to you, what size would you like it?

Is your next mate an experienced Don Juan or a Novice Ned? Is your sexual experience a good measure to your mates?

How do your religious beliefs about sex guide you with sexual experiences? There are many books out there on sex in relationships, sexual positions, even on the romance of sex. What are your feelings about sex? Are you comfortable speaking about sex with your mate? Was sex taboo in your home when you were growing up or was it spoken about like any other topic?

The Don Juan type is very experienced in romance and sex and uses his amazing talents to the utmost to please a woman. Unfortunately, you may not be the only woman he is pleasing. Could you handle having your mate craving to please other women as he pleases you? What if he takes the desire to the next level?

The Novice Ned type needs a teacher to show him the ropes. If you are the *in-charge* type this might be the type for you. Is your student eager to learn new tricks? Is your student a quick learner? Can your student take what he has learned and apply the knowledge? Will you get tired of teaching all the time and just want to be ravished by a Don Juan type now and then?

All our past sexual experiences matter when it comes to future ones and so do those of your mate. Sex is usually one of the biggest parts of a relationship. So, you might wish to create the sexual stud you desire in the next pages and see how soon he comes knocking at your door.

Take a Mental Moment to create the sexual stud you want and see who comes busting through your door for that passionate first kiss. He is starting to shape up quite nicely!

His Sex-perience

Infidelity to my mate is:

> looking at the opposite sex   hitting on the opposite sex
> kissing another man/woman
> having oral sex with someone other than him
> having sexual intercourse with someone besides him
> dreaming of someone other than him
> Other_____
>
> _____

My mate is:

> for open relationships   jealous in a relationship
> a one-woman man   could live without me
> happiest in a relationship
> Other_____
>
> _____

The definition of sex for my mate is:

> kissing   hugging   holding hands   watching
> porn   oral sex   actual intercourse
> fetishes   lusting thoughts   bondage
> Other_____
>
> _____

Manifest Your Mate

My mate loves to_____ after we have sex:

> cuddle   shower   watch T.V.   smoke
> watch me fall asleep   fall asleep   tell me he
> loves me   walk the dog   eat something
> Other_____
>
> _____

My mate expresses love by:

> having sex   love letters   romantic getaways
> Hallmark cards   surprises   I love You
> turning on the TV   turning on the radio
> giving me the remote   massaging my feet
> Other_____
>
> _____

My mate must have sex:

> every day   every hour   twice a day   in the shower
> in public   wearing a costume   wearing make-up
> wearing a uniform
> Other_____
>
> _____

My mate prefers:

> me to be on top   rough sex   sexual aids
> the lights on   the lights off   to watch
> multiple partners   cuffs

Other_____

_____

Foreplay to my mate is:

"Hey, Honey, I'm home"   timed   not for them

a spanking   heavy kissing   always interesting

watching porn   sex

Other_____

_____

My mate learned everything they know about sex from:

their mother   their father   their sibling   movies

magazines   school   practice   porn flicks

the girl/boy down the block   practice

Other_____

_____

My mate:

talks my ear off during sex   likes silent sex

is open for anything   has a favorite song for sex

speaks soft erotic words in my ear

has an applause track they play afterwards

makes funny noises

Other_____

_____

Take a Mental Moment. Take a breath. Close your eyes and imagine the first time you have sex with your new mate. How does it start? Is it romantic? Is it passionate? How do you feel when he enters you? How do you feel after the act?

_____

_____

_____

_____

_____

_____

_____

_____

_____

_____

_____

_____

_____

_____

_____

_____

_____

_____

_____

_____

_____

_____

Meaningful Memories or Triggers

_____

_____

_____

_____

_____

_____

_____

_____

_____

_____

_____

_____

_____

_____

_____

_____

_____

_____

_____

_____

_____

_____

_____

_____

_____

What My Dreams Say

Use these pages to follow your dreams while creating your mate. Dreams are very powerful connections into your deepest self and the universe. You may be surprised by the information you collect on your soon to be delivered mate.

_____

_____

_____

_____

_____

_____

_____

_____

_____

_____

_____

_____

_____

_____

_____

_____

_____

_____

_____

_____

SEX-perience Counts

_____

_____

_____

_____

_____

_____

_____

_____

_____

_____

_____

_____

_____

_____

_____

_____

_____

_____

_____

_____

_____

_____

_____

_____

_____

_____

_____

Important Notes & Questions

You may think of some questions that are not in this book. Keeping track of them when you think of them will benefit you in creating your mate.

_____

_____

_____

_____

_____

_____

_____

_____

_____

_____

_____

_____

_____

_____

_____

_____

_____

_____

_____

_____

_____

_____

SEX-perience Counts

"If you don't stick to your values when they're being tested, they're not values: they're hobbies."

Jon Stewart

Hobbies, Sports & Interests

Having things in common, to fill up empty time and experience new things with each other, is a necessity to keep a relationship going strong and growing together instead of apart. My image of a strong relationship is one of a ladder. The two sides are the two individuals. Each strong and capable of standing on their own without the other. The rungs between them are the bonds that keep them together. Some rungs may fall away through the term of the relationship but if the rungs that stay are solid, the relationship will stand the tests of time.

Men are usually very physically oriented and anything with a ball, tires or tits, will grab their attention. They are quick to do whatever it takes to instigate a gathering around events that pertain to the list above. Hopefully your tits will suffice for that interest but a titty bar now and then may be on your man's secret activity list. However, balls, used in golf, tennis, basketball, baseball, football, soccer and billiards are round things that will take up some of their spare time and hopefully not all of it.

So, what *ball* interests do you have besides the ones hanging between your new mate's legs? Taking up an activity or two that involves any ball, will certainly give you an advantage when it comes to participating with your mate in these hobbies or sports. Taking a few lessons in tennis, golf or billiards may even have you meeting some great guys. Honing skills that are valuable rungs on your ladder to a strong solid relationship with your new mate.

Mutual interests like, painting, wood working, music, electronics, collecting, cooking, theater, etc., are great ways to bond and create rungs with your mate. It may give you, or your mate, an outlet for expression and reflection. What are some of your interests? Does your mate share any? What do the two of you having in common as far as hobbies or sports? Does he like to entertain? Travel?

Take a Mental Moment and imagine all the things you two share in sports, hobbies and interests. Imagine how you feel when you see the two of you doing these things together. Are you thankful that you have found your perfect mate? Then shout it out. Or make a drawing of your feelings in the space below.

Hobbies, Sports & Interests

His Hobbies/Sports/Interests

My mate has:

      several hobbies   too many hobbies
      the same hobbies as me
      no hobbies   wants to discover one together
      Other_____

_____

My mate likes:

      softball   baseball   football   soccer   tennis
      golf   sex   basketball   hockey   volleyball
      water polo   gymnastics
      Other_____

_____

My mate plays in a league for:

      softball   baseball   soccer   tennis
      golf   basketball   hockey   bowling
      billiards   fantasy football
      Other_____

_____

My mate must watch sports programming:

      any time a game is on   once a week   finals only
      at a sports bar   with his buddies
      all weekend long   in his man cave
      Other_____

_____

Manifest Your Mate

My mate watches:

drag racing   Indy 500   Nascar   Demolition Derby
Tour de France   motocross   Grand Prix   traffic
Other_____

My mate participates in:

motocross   classic car rallies   muscle car meets
selling cars   cross country touring   fixing cars
buying cars   cycling
Other_____

My mate has a passion for:

classic films   modern art   ancient artifacts
classic novels   movie posters   classical music
operas   jazz festivals   rock&roll   costume parties
rap concerts   Broadway shows   gambling
the horse track   the zoo   museums
Other_____

My mate collects:

nothing   dust   everything   snow globes   old tools
classic cars   sports paraphernalia   movie posters
leather bound books   coins postage stamps
classic motorcycles   ink pens   watches
unique experiences   friends   money
Other_____

My mate de-stresses by:

    painting   smoking weed   drinking   writing
    boxing   being creative in some way
    watching TV   working out
    going to the shooting range   listening to classical
    music   sex
    Other_____

_____

My mate plays:

    the piano   guitar   drums   saxophone   cello
    violin   the field   flute   harmonica
    spoons   cards   games
    Other_____

_____

My mate likes to read:

    short stories   novels   non-fiction   fiction
    comic books   phone books   educational
    books   newspaper   posts & tweets
    Other_____

_____

Take a moment. Take a breath. Close your eyes and imagine doing things you like with your mate. Do you see yourself playing sports with him? What interests are you sharing? Any common hobbies? How do you feel when you share this kind of time with him?

_____

_____

_____

_____

_____

_____

_____

_____

_____

_____

_____

_____

_____

_____

Meaningful Memories or Triggers

What My Dreams Say

Use these pages to follow your dreams while creating your mate. Dreams are very powerful connections into your deepest self and the universe. You may be surprised by the information you collect on your soon to be delivered mate.

_____

_____

_____

_____

_____

_____

_____

_____

_____

_____

_____

_____

_____

_____

_____

_____

_____

_____

_____

Hobbies, Sports & Interests

Important Notes & Questions

You may think of some questions that are not in this book. Keeping track of them when you think of them will benefit you in creating your mate.

Hobbies, Sports & Interests

"People who want to share their religious views with you, almost never want you to share yours with them."

Dave Barry

Family, Values and Religion

How we are raised creates a basis in our beliefs that can carry through one's entire life. The family environment is an important aspect to look at when you meet someone. If his family life was not like yours, the differences in how you both work through things could be vast. If the values instilled in your mate are not the ones instilled in you, conflict could arise in many areas. Especially when it comes to raising children. The religion his parents chose to expose him to has molded his views. Your mate's religious beliefs may be very strict or non-existent or somewhere between. Do they vibrate with yours?

Are you looking for someone who shares your same values or values that could serve you in making changes you wish to make in yourself? Are you looking for someone who had a rough childhood or one that was *normal*? Are you strict when it comes to your religious viewpoints? Would you be open to raising your children under your mate's religion, if it differs from yours? Where do you draw the line when it comes to moral values?

There are different family structures. One type is—solid as a rock—where family is everything, even though the foundation of it is broken. Traditions and holidays hold them together and everyone is *nice* when they gather. Then there are those other types: those that never see each other; those who must contact their mother every day; those that have set holiday and birthday gatherings that will never be changed. Where do you fit in these with your beliefs and family traditions? How would you blend yours with your mate's?

Let's say you are Christian and your mate is Jewish. His family goes to synagogue every Saturday and your family goes to church every Sunday. Do you make a pact that both of you will participate equally in each family's traditions? Does this mean that Saturday and Sunday is occupied with synagogue and church? Or do you do your thing and he does his? Good things to think about when committing to a relationship or marriage.

What about holidays? Do you go home every Thanksgiving? Does your mate? How would you handle Thanksgiving if you both go home and those homes are not near the each other? Sometimes these choices can drive deep wedges between families. How would his family expect the holiday traditions to happen? Do you care what your family expects? Are you past the stage of having to visit for the holidays? Do you vacation away from family at holidays to avoid seeing them or having to endure the pain?

Are your religious beliefs set in stone or would you be open to explore other religions if your mate desired you to do so? Would you convert your religion for your mate? Would you expect your mate to convert to your religion? Does religion matter to you in a relationship? Religious values, encoded since childhood, can sometimes be hard to overlook when it comes to accepting someone else's point of view. There is a beautiful film by Barry Levinson, *Avalon,* that shows how a family changes through generations of holidays. How travel and work in modern America, leaves no time for traditional family gatherings.

Take a Mental Moment and imagine your first conversation about religion with your mate. How do you feel with him in this moment? Imagine your first holiday together that involves family and envision how that experience goes down. How do you feel about your choice?

His Views on Family, Values & Religion

My mate was born:

> to a single mom   to a married couple
> orphaned at birth   and put up for adoption at birth
> out of wedlock
> Other_____

My mate's parents:

> are stilled married   are divorced   one is deceased
> both are deceased   are of the same sex
> both are remarried
> Other_____

My mate was raised:

> Catholic   Christian   Jewish   Buddhist
> Hindu   Atheist   Mormon   Muslim
> Non-denominational
> Other_____

My mate takes religion:

> very seriously   seriously   doesn't care
> practices at holidays   only when parents are in town
> as ridiculous   as a tradition
> Other_____

My mate currently:

> doesn't follow a religion   believes in God
> believes in Christ   believes in himself
> believes in a higher power   is a scientist
> believes in the Evolution theory
> believes the Creationist theory
> does not believe there is a Higher Power
> Other_____

When my mate was younger in his family, he:

> ate dinner together when Dad got home
> went to sleepovers   had sleepovers   had chores
> did his homework with his siblings right after school
> had an allowance
> Other_____

My mate's parents were:

> very strict disciplinarians   verbally abusive   hippy like
> physically abusive   never raised their voice to the
> children   very loving   understanding
> Other_____

My mate was raised:

> in a big city   in a small town   in a suburb
> on a farm   in a foreign country   in a commune
> in an orphanage   by his grand parents
> Other_____

Manifest Your Mate

Growing up, my mate had:

older brothers   older sisters   younger brothers
no siblings   younger sisters   step siblings
adopted siblings   pets
Other_____

_____

My mate thinks marriage is:

the last resort   the next step   a waste of time
not necessary to show your love   a tradition
a prison   a business   a must for having kids
a rip off   not needed to raise kids
Other_____

_____

My mate thinks divorce is:

never going to happen to him   the next step
the last resort   evil admitting failure   sacrilegious
the easy way to fix things   a business
something he would never grant   reason to party
Other_____

_____

My mate grew up seeing his parents:

hug and kiss openly   argue in front of him
cheating on each other   lie to each other
express love to him openly   naked a lot
sad   lose their jobs   in love all the time   happy
get divorced
Other_____

_____

Family, Values & Religion

In a relationship. my mate thinks it is important to:

be alone a lot   be together most the time
travel for work   be apart 50% of the time
have a house full of people all the time
have separate bedrooms   have separate bathrooms
play
Other_____

In a relationship, my mate thinks PDA means:

put down arms   public display of affection
pretty damn accurate   personal digital assistant
please don't arrest   it's ok to have sex in public
kissing in public   holding hands in the park
Other_____

My mate is comfortable with telling me:

when he thinks I am inappropriate   I look great
he needs a break   he would prefer I do it his way
he made a mistake   I Love You   he needs alone
time   he needs a hug   he needs sex
Other_____

If we had children together, my mate would want us to:

raise them following a religion   home school
send them to a private school   have boys only
teach them many religions   have girls only
send them off to boarding school   have more than 3
Other_____

Take a moment. Take a breath. Close your eyes and imagine how it feels when the two of you have a family. How does it feels to be with his family? How does it feel to be silent yet in each other's company? Imagine how it feels to grow old with this man. How many kids do you have? Imagine holidays together.

_____

_____

_____

_____

_____

_____

_____

_____

_____

_____

_____

_____

_____

_____

_____

_____

_____

_____

Meaningful Memories or Triggers

_____

_____

_____

_____

_____

_____

_____

_____

_____

_____

_____

_____

_____

_____

_____

_____

_____

_____

_____

_____

_____

_____

_____

What My Dreams Say

Use these pages to follow your dreams while creating your mate. Dreams are very powerful connections into your deepest self and the universe. You may be surprised by the information you collect on your soon to be delivered mate.

_____

_____

_____

_____

_____

_____

_____

_____

_____

_____

_____

_____

_____

_____

_____

_____

_____

_____

_____

Family, Values & Religion

Important Notes & Questions

You may think of some questions that are not in this book. Keeping track of them when you think of them will benefit you in creating your mate.

Family, Values & Religion

"Big jobs usually go to men who prove their ability to outgrow small ones."

Theodore Roosevelt

Education, Finances & Politics

Now your mate has taken on an appearance, personality and profession. You created his interests, know about his family, values and his religious beliefs. This character of your imagination is quite an amazing find now.

You know his track record in many areas as well as how he is in the sack! Good job thus far. You have probably even had some encounters with men that hold many of the qualities you have thought about. Have any of them piqued your interest? Are any realistic candidates? Do you need to weed through any of these charming possibilities? Maybe the guy is still trying to find you. Maybe your creative skills have left out a few more identifying aspects that, when written down, will send one last signal for your creation to arrive in your life.

Education stands high on a lot of people's list for qualities they wish in their mate. Most feel that a college degree is the least they would settle for because they believe this means that the guy will land a job and keep it. Not necessarily true. However, an educational experience beyond high school gives one the chance—to *grow up*, *be responsible* and *become an adult*. Of course, all that happens if the person has left home during that four-year period. The bonds made with new people, the way one chooses to learn, the responsibilities one takes on during these years all help create who they become in their adult life.

Education and finances are certainly not linked anymore, like they used to be. Having an education is no guarantee for a high paying job. Song writers, celebrities and other professions of that sort don't usually need an education. Musicians, artists and writers certainly don't need an education to garner the finances they bring in. So, thinking with a broader stroke, you can allow your created mate to have great financial abundance with or without an education.

Fixating on making money or having to have money is draining and worrisome on a couple. Although money is needed, in society as it is now, it certainly does not make the world go around. It is probably not the reason we are all on this planet. What is it you want in your mate? Does he need to have a certain level of education? Does he need to have a salary that meets a certain sum? Will he be the bread winner?

Common advice—never bring up politics! I feel that one's political affiliation affects how one thinks about a lot of issues and can be a deal breaker in a relationship. If one is radically Left or radically Right, there is no meeting of the minds. If one's political inclination is more central, there is room for leaning Left or Right on issues. Nothing is black or white. Everything is shades of colors. Do you think you could live with someone whose political beliefs were in strong opposition to yours? Could you live with someone who has polar opposite religious beliefs?

Does your new mate believe that everything should be free? How does he think the *free* stuff appears or is had? Does your new mate believe that everyone should be responsible for themselves and earn their own way, no matter what? What happens when he falls on hard times?

Take a Mental Moment and give your mate an education that could carry you through financially troubled times. Enhance him with financial abundance and wisdom to further his and your existence. He is almost a complete person in your eyes by now. He is well on his way to being in your life for a long time.

Manifest Your Mate

His Views on Education, Financial & Politics

My mate's highest level of education is:

> high school   college no degree   college with degree
> Other_____

The college degree my mate has, is a/an:

> Associate   Master's   Bachelor's   PhD
> Other_____

My mate thinks education is:

> a waste of time   brainwashing   a lifelong profession
> a must   a great way to meet woman
> necessary to get a job   babysitting
> Other_____

My mate went to a/an:

> State University   Ivy League College
> Community college   night school while working
> Foreign University   online school
> Other_____

My mate had his education paid for:

> by his parents   by student loans   by scholarship
> by a trust fund   by his ex-wife   he is still paying for it
> by his grandparents   by his employer

Other_____

_____

My mate thinks this is sufficient USA income for him to bring home:

25-50,000   35,000-75,000   50,000-100,000
75,000-150,000   100,000 to 200,000
over 200,000   over 1 million
Other_____

_____

My mate would expect:

me to bring home a salary equal to his
me not to work
would hope I had a trust fund or pension
would want me to work so I had outside interests
would never expect me to work if we had kids
would pay me a salary for the work I do around the
house and for raising the children
Other_____

_____

My mate's parents:

were wealthy   are wealthy   are in deep debt
are bankers   give him a monthly amount to live on
are accountants   have a fund for grandchildren
are running from the IRS
Other_____

_____

Manifest Your Mate

My mate would:

        have no trouble getting on government assistance
        would stay on government assistance
        never take a hand out
        has never heard of a hand out
        knows when he needs financial help way in advance
        always have a mom and/or dad to fall back on
        Other_____

_____

My mate:

        can openly discuss his financial issues
        always relies on his parents to get him out of a bind
        would have a financial advisor   is an accountant
        is a financial advisor   has unlimited finances

        Other_____

_____

My mate believes children should:

        earn their way at a certain age   always be kids
        have an allowance   study hard in school
        learn about saving at an early age
        follow the stock market   have a college fund
        Other_____

_____

My mate's political environment growing up was one of:

        Conservatism   Liberalism   Centralism
        Anarchism   Communism   Fascism   Socialism
        Other_____

_____

My mate's political inclination is:

Conservatism   Liberalism   Centralism
Anarchism   Communism Fascism   Socialism
Other_____

_____

My mate's political views are:

strict   unwavering   swinging   set in stone
the same as his parents   open to change
that the system is broken   he doesn't vote
Other_____

_____

My mate believes one should:

vote their party no matter what   not vote
          listen to all sides then decide
vote against a party   think hard before voting
Other_____

_____

My mate thinks politics are:

a way to divide the populous   corrupt
    a necessity   honest   a joke
a way to divert attention from important issues and
events
Other_____

_____

Take a moment. Take a breath. Close your eyes and imagine how it feels to know about your mates' educational choices, successes, failures and his financial situation now and when you are together. Do you feel safe in all his decisions? Do you feel the need to—*be in charge*—of the finances? Are you ok with his political views?

_____

_____

_____

_____

_____

_____

_____

_____

_____

_____

_____

_____

_____

_____

_____

_____

_____

_____

_____

_____

Meaningful Memories or Triggers

What My Dreams Say

Again, use these pages to follow your dreams while creating your mate. Dreams are very powerful connections into your deepest self and the universe. You may be surprised by the information you collect on your soon to be delivered mate.

_____

_____

_____

_____

_____

_____

_____

_____

_____

_____

_____

_____

_____

_____

_____

_____

_____

_____

_____

_____

_____

_____

Education, Finances & politics

Important Notes & Questions

When considering education, finances and politics, you may think of some questions that are not in this book. Keeping track of them when you think of them will benefit you in creating your mate and give you a space to save important questions to ask him when you have discussions on these topics.

_____

_____

_____

_____

_____

_____

_____

_____

_____

_____

_____

_____

_____

_____

_____

_____

_____

_____

Education, Finances & politics

"Me and my husband lived happily for twenty years...and then we met."

Anonymous

Marriage & Commitment

Up until recently, society and cultural preferences have painted a path that leads to marriage and commitment when two people fall into a romantic relationship. Most couples will end up with some sort of promise to each other that usually involves making vows to each other in the witness of family and friends, a judge and/or a religious representative. This is commonly called a marriage.

Often thousands of dollars are spent on an elaborate marriage ceremony customarily paid for by the family of the bride, *wife-to-be*. In certain cultures, marriages are arranged between families without the wife-to-be or husband-to-be having any say in the matter. These are arranged marriages.

The concept of—happily ever after—seems to vanish when it comes to marriage, depending on where you live. Belgium has the highest rate of divorce at 71%. The USA has a rate of 53%. In these countries, marriages are a choice between the people making the union. However, most marriages in the world are arranged marriages. 55% of marriages are arranged and of those only 6% end in divorce. Does this mean that arranged is better than having a choice? No. The countries that promote arranged marriages have rules and reasons as to why the divorce rate is so low, which are particular to each country or religion. These reasons may have nothing to do with the happiness of either marriage partner.

No matter what the marriage circumstance is at the time of the union, people change. It is those changes, and how the marriage was structured to handle them, that will eventually lead to success or failure when the hurdles of life appear. If one waltzes into marriage, because they are in love with the other person, what happens if that other person has an affair? Besides the betrayal that is felt, should one stay in that union? Will it happen again? If it does, what is the next step? Is it important? Does it matter that trust is broken? Can it be mended?

Some people marry for tax benefits, others for insurance purposes and some considered legally married after a certain time of living together. In any aspect of this sort of union, certain legal rights are immediate upon the signing of a marriage license. Making the union a legal entity, governed by laws of the state and country where the couple reside.

The people who decide to jump into a marriage should be informed about what that means legally. If a divorce happens, the state treats the husband and wife as legal partners in a *partnership*. The courts then follow procedure for the *dissolution* of a marriage as they would any other legal partnership structure. Many couples arrange a prenuptial agreement before they marry. This clarifies and expresses, while they are—in love—what they wish to happen in the event of divorce. This *prenup* can be a good tool for financial, emotional and psychological reasons.

Marriage is a business! Look at all the money that usually goes into one. The wedding gown, the invitations, the ceremony, the honeymoon and the gifts. Big business. If you are in love with someone and they wish to commit to you, they can do so without marriage. Modern times, especially in the western countries, accept children born out-of-wedlock. Sex is usually experienced way before a marriage, in many countries throughout the world. Couples can live together without fear of being outcasts in society. Children are no longer ridiculed because their parents aren't married.

When looking for a commitment or marriage from your mate, will you insist on a prenuptial agreement? Why or why not? Would you be willing to sign a prenup if your mate presented you one? Would you have an attorney look it over and revise it to meet your expectations? Would you follow the traditional path of—blind love—and marry with no plan set in place for the tough times?

Take a Mental Moment and create the perfect *business plan* for your commitment to succeed. Your mate is very close to arriving at your door, if he hasn't already and this last step may find you waltzing down the aisle of your dreams.

His Views on Marriage & Commitment

In a committed relationship, my mate believes in:

getting married   being together, but living separately
living together
Other_____

_____

My mate would:

want to move into my place
want me to move into his place
expect me to move in with him at his parents' home
want us to have our own places
have many places together
Other_____

_____

My mate would expect:

a civil ceremony   an elaborate religious ceremony
no ceremony   fun spiritual ceremony
me to make the decision and plans
a whacky ceremony   his parents to tell him what to do
Other_____

_____

If trouble arose in our marriage, my mate would:

run away   be the one to call a therapist
expect me to fix it   call his mom
hug me and tell me "We can get through this".
file for divorce

Other_____

_____

My mate thinks commitment is:

    forever   for as long as we are both happy
    until death do we part   until the kids are 18
    for as long as he is happy   for as long as I am happy
    until the kids are 18
    Other_____

_____

My mate believes a marriage ceremony is/ is something:

    you do to keep your woman happy
    a waste of time   a commitment to God
    you do to have kids   a waste of money
    a reason for a big party   a reason to dress up
    you do to make your mom happy
    a way to express his love
    Other_____

_____

If I chose to wait to have sex until we were married, my mate would:

    get a new girlfriend   have women on the side
    agree with me   call the courthouse
    book the Elvis chapel   think I was crazy
    introduce me to someone else   be very frustrated
    Other_____

_____

Take a Mental Moment. Take a breath. Close your eyes and imagine your union, marriage or ceremony of commitment with your mate. Where is it? Who is attending? What does he say to you? How do you feel when you hear those words?

_____

_____

_____

_____

_____

_____

_____

_____

_____

_____

_____

_____

_____

_____

_____

_____

_____

Meaningful Memories or Triggers

_____

_____

_____

_____

_____

_____

_____

_____

_____

_____

_____

_____

_____

_____

_____

_____

_____

What My Dreams Say

More space for you to record your dreams while creating your mate. Dreams are very powerful connections into your deepest self and the universe. You may be surprised by the information you collect on your soon to be delivered mate.

_____

_____

_____

_____

_____

_____

_____

_____

_____

_____

_____

_____

_____

_____

_____

_____

_____

_____

_____

Marriage & Commitment

Important Notes & Questions

Questions will most certainly pop into your head that are not in this book. Marriage is a major step in a relationship. Here is more space for you to put them down when they arise. A note place for you to return to when your mate enters your life.

_____

_____

_____

_____

_____

_____

_____

_____

_____

_____

_____

_____

_____

_____

_____

_____

_____

_____

Marriage & Commitment

Part Three

It's about TIME

"Men are like a fine wine. They start out like grapes, and it's our job to stomp on them and keep them in the dark until they mature into something you'd like to have dinner with."

Author Unknown

Creation Compilation

Bravo! You have just broadcast the energy necessary to create the mate of your desires. In this section, you will have space to compile all the traits and aspects you chose, filled in or imagined. All in one place, to quickly review. Again, the more you write it down the more energy you send across the ether. Affecting your man and causing him to head in your direction.

In this section, you can add or remove, focus on important traits and/or be more specific on any one. You are the artist, painter and writer. You are creating the character of your mate and directing the Universe to quickly and effectively deliver your order.

Doubt is the eraser of desire. So, have no doubt that your wishes and commands will come to you. Faith is the initiator of reality and your thoughts are the director of your production.

Take a moment and write on the following pages all the aspects you have noted thus far. This is a quick and easy reference area to come to as you sift through the men that coming to your life.

Physical Traits

_____

_____

_____

_____

_____

_____

_____

_____

_____

_____

_____

_____

_____

_____

_____

_____

_____

_____

_____

_____

_____

_____

_____

_____

_____

_____

_____

Who They Are

_____

_____

_____

_____

_____

_____

_____

_____

_____

_____

_____

_____

_____

_____

_____

_____

_____

_____

_____

_____

_____

_____

_____

_____

_____

Profession

_____
_____
_____
_____
_____
_____
_____
_____
_____
_____
_____
_____
_____
_____
_____
_____
_____
_____
_____
_____
_____
_____
_____
_____

Track Record

SEX-perience Counts

_____

_____

_____

_____

_____

_____

_____

_____

_____

_____

_____

_____

_____

_____

_____

_____

_____

_____

_____

_____

_____

_____

_____

_____

_____

Hobbies / Sports / Interests

Family, Values & Religion

Education, Finances & Politics

_____

_____

_____

_____

_____

_____

_____

_____

_____

_____

_____

_____

_____

_____

_____

_____

_____

_____

_____

_____

_____

_____

_____

_____

_____

_____

_____

_____

_____

_____

Marriage & Commitment

_____
_____
_____
_____
_____
_____
_____
_____
_____
_____
_____
_____
_____
_____
_____
_____
_____
_____
_____
_____
_____
_____
_____
_____

"Plant the seed of desire in your mind and it forms a nucleus with power to attract to itself everything needed for its fulfillment."

Robert Collier

What Are You Willing To Do?

Now you have the perfect guy at hand! Are you ready for him?

You might have asked yourself some questions along the way. Hopefully you wrote them in the *Notes & Questions* sections or other blank spaces in this book. Now is the time to look back and gather any notes that may lead you to your next step. What are you willing to do when you meet him?

The Universe will deliver exactly what you asked for. It is time to take some action. Have you noticed any new friends in your life? Have some fallen away? Have you changed jobs or wanted to? Have you been forced to leave your living arrangement? Have you planned any trips?

The shifts that happen in us during creation phases are subtle or abrupt. Sometimes they seem like our world is turning upside down. At other times, they seem as gifts and are a daily occurrence. One's attitude toward change can greatly affect how these experiences are welcomed or shunned away. Remember that the Universe will make your creation and desires happen in the ways it can, not the ways you may want. This means that change, whether perceived as good or bad, may happen to allow you and your new mate to meet.

Have good friends or co-workers suggested you meet someone they know? Have you been invited to more events recently? Have you been put in situations where you are out-of-town or state? If your mate lives in another state or country, of course the Universe might have to get you together by relocating you or causing an unexpected opportunity. This can happen through work, vacation, girls' weekends or even loss. Hopefully you have taken advantage of these opportunities for change and have an updated passport.

Take a Mental Moment. Take a breath and list five things that you would be willing to do to meet your mate.

_____

_____

_____

_____

_____

_____

_____

_____

_____

_____

_____

_____

What Are You Willing To Do?

_____

_____

_____

_____

_____

_____

_____

_____

"Good sex is like good bridge. If you don't have a good partner you better have a good hand."

Mae West

1st Questions You Would Ask?

Let's get serious for a moment! The impressions of a first date or meeting will guide you to the next date or another person. Every man you meet is a potential mate. Look back at your casual history of dating or meeting men. How have the conversations usually started? What type of opening question sparks your attention the most? What is *your* best opening line?

If you are serious about meeting your mate, based upon the explorations and statements you made in this journal, what will your first question be to him? Even though, when asking it, you don't know it is him yet. The response to your opening line should definitely let you know this is the guy the Universe has sent you based on your criteria. What is the most important thing you could ask that would let you know this is him? You can set that question and response up now so that you know this is the guy.

It's just like the rest of the intention work you are doing here. No different. It's like giving yourself a sign to look for when you meet him.

Sometimes we need a sign. Our daily routine and life can get in our way of being aware every minute. We are only human after all. So be as playful and daring as you want and create a *sign*. One that will make you acutely aware that the man standing in front of you, listening and responding to you with your exact pre-destined response, is someone worth paying attention to. A huge smile might creep across your face when you realize this. Which will only make him more responsive and interested.

Because we are only human, we may doubt ourselves or the situation. Have a follow-up question ready with a follow-up response to make sure that this is the guy. So, that you don't waste time if he isn't. Go ahead and create interesting opening lines or questions and responses that he would say.

Here is an example. My question. "Do you suppose life is a game?" His response. "Artificial turf." That would get my attention. Another example. My Question. "What does love feel like?" His response. "Clouds."

Take a Mental Moment. Take a breath and list five opening lines and/or questions that you would say or ask and the responses that your possible mate would reply with, that would give you a heads-up, that this is the guy.

_____

_____

_____

_____

_____

_____

_____

_____

1st Questions You Would Ask

_____

_____

_____

_____

_____

_____

_____

_____

_____

_____

_____

_____

Pick up line

Do you believe in love at first sight, or should I walk by again?

His First Words

You are out with some friends at a gallery opening, sipping a glass of wine and nibbling on a smear of cheese on a cracker. You're admiring a red square painting on a stark white wall. Your thoughts race from the flavor of the wine, the taste of the cheese to the reason the artist chose that shade and shape. Your mind is searching for meaning in the entire experience. You seek the reason you came to this event in the first place. Was it the cheese, the wine, the art? Or that you would never meet Mr. Right sitting at home in front of your television?

In the solace of our minds, thoughts are racing all the time. Even now as your eyes ingest and decipher this code of text your mind is wandering around. That is fine, if one of them is what the first words out of your new mate's mouth be, when he approaches you.

You can probably surmise what your new mate would say to you, based upon what you have logged thus far.

Defining a question or statement, is no different from imagining the color of his hair or how he smiles. Is the first thing he would say to you a question? A statement. A remark about something? Does it make you laugh? Ponder? Or cry? Is it quirky? Is it political? Is it sarcastic?

It could even be silent! It could be a gesture. It could be a look. It could be an action. Try to imagine what it is that will make you aware that this guy needs your immediate attention. I meditated on this and came up with some strange opening lines that made no sense, but would alert and engage me.

Here are different examples. He stands on a tabletop in a restaurant. He says. "I prefer green apples to red". He gives you a seashell. He mentions Gang-104 from *One Day in the Life of Ivan Denisovich* by Alexander Solzhenitsyn.

Take a Mental Moment. Take a breath and list five opening lines and/or questions that your new mate would say or ask you that when you hear, you will know this is him. He might even do something instead of say something that would give you the clue.

_____

_____

_____

_____

_____

_____

_____

_____

_____

_____

_____

_____

_____

_____

_____

Circle five words from the list below that your created mate will describe you as, to his friends after your first date.

Stressed	Responsible	Healthy
Gifted	Dramatic	Calm
Average	Strong	Intelligent
Loving	Joyful	Humorous
Brave	Selfless	Passionate
Wise	Emotional	Great kisser
Helpful	Peaceful	Perfect for me
Fearful	Compassionate	Timid
Messy	Grounded	Wild
Shining	Unpredictable	Late

His First Words

"The first time you buy a house you see how pretty the paint is and buy it. The second time you look to see if the basement has termites. It's the same with men."

Lupe Velez

Top 20 Must Haves - Must Be

You have created your perfect mate! You have probably met several men by now who fit the criteria you've noted in this journal. You may date a few of these men at the same time, to see who meets all your needs and desires.

You may feel uncertain of getting involved with one or more of these potential mates. Looking back in this journal is a good way to keep on track with your original desires. When you find yourself confused, about your intentions, open it again. You may change your mind after having sex with any of these men. Sex can confuse or alter desires. He may meet most of your criteria and fall short in an area that means a lot to you.

Having a scale of the most important qualities you are looking for is beneficial now. Long ago, an acquaintance of mine came to me with a list of twenty things he needed in his partner. He met someone and was considering marriage. He showed me the list. At that time, I never met anyone who knew exactly what they wanted in a partner and what they would settle for. I found it interesting. He proceeded to tell me that the woman he met had many of the qualities listed on the paper but not two of the five most important—must haves / must be—on his list. They ended up getting married anyway. Had two kids. Got involved in businesses together. They seemed happy.

Then one day, his wife announced to me that he had left her for another woman. His wife was unaware that I knew about the list and the two qualities that she lacked that were important to her ex. I asked her why she thought he left her and pursued the other woman? After all, the other woman was not much younger than his wife and had children the same age as his. Her reasoning was that he was a philanderer and this wasn't this first time. She mentioned that she had their second child to make the marriage better.

I knew differently. I wondered if his wife knew what the qualities were that she lacked. And if she did, would she try to change them to keep the marriage together? Is it possible to change the core of who we are? Whether we're changing for ourselves or someone else? Should we expect a person can change or should change? If we make a list of the top things we must have in a mate or that our mate must be or do, would we stick to it? Should we?

I think it is a great idea! Especially if one has had several relationships that have not been what they expected or that have ended in divorce or disaster. Could it possibly be that the relationship was entered with expectations of changing the other person?

Take a Mental Moment to realize the top twenty qualities that your mate must have or must be. Jot them down here in pencil. They can be numbered after they are written down.

_____

_____

_____

_____

_____

Top 20 Must Haves – Must Be

_____

_____

_____

_____

_____

_____

_____

_____

_____

_____

_____

_____

_____

_____

_____

_____

_____

"Thought, ORGANIZED, is the greatest power in the world."

Hashnu O'Hara

Your Order Has Shipped

The steps and processes you have just finished have broadcast a strong frequency of desire. The Universe and all the players involved with the delivery of your order are on a subtle level. One by one, each participant will take action to ensure that your package arrives exactly as you instructed. They may not know why they are taking these steps, but you will, if you stay aware during this process. Be alert for signals sent directly from the Universe through your inner senses. Take note if your friends, family or coworkers have a desire to introduce you to someone they think you will like. Be open to unexpected trips, relocations or invites to events that you would never have thought to attend. Take close look at e-mails you receive during this time, they will hold clues and offer guidance.

The Universe works in mysterious ways! The ego—*you*—thinks it has control over how things will manifest. It doesn't, therefore you don't either. It is time to *know*, inside your heart, that what you have just created will emerge in your life by the date you write. On the next pages, you will find a sample Universal Commands as well as one where you can fill in the blanks that pertain to your intentions. Be as precise as you can. Being specific will get you what you ask for faster than being vague.

Once you place your order you must have no doubt, as doubt is an eraser of dreams. This is time to act as if you have this man in your life. If you are lazy about how you dress or tend to your appearance, now is a good time to pay attention to how you look or how your appearance may attract or deter. Start attending events, getting out of your house, putting yourself in places or situations where you think can meet your mate. Unless you are having constant massive repairs done on your home, it is unlikely you will meet him by staying in the house. You could start saying *yes* to everything.

Imagination plus feelings creates a reality. Imagine now that you are laying on a warm sunny beach in the Caribbean. Once you have that in your mind's eye, sense how you feel as you lay there? What do you hear? What do you smell? Use all your senses. Now become aware of any physical sensations you are experiencing. You might feel, calm, warmth and peaceful. You may smile as you hear the seagulls or see a small crab dig under the sand to avoid you.

Now, place yourself on a cold frozen lakeshore. See in your minds' eye the terrain around you. Feel the frozen air as it rushes across your face. Take you attention to your feet. Are they warm or cold in this setting? Are you relaxed? Do you need of another layer of clothing to feel comfortable? How do you feel when you are standing there? Do you feel different from the warm shore of the sea?

If you experienced any feelings in the above situations, then you can realize—your thoughts affect change in the physical world. It is no different from what you just accomplished in this book. Your thoughts have also created a change in the physical world of the Universe. You may take time now to go over any chapters and revise, add or remove some of your requests. Also, review the *What My Dreams Say* and *Important Notes & Questions* sections before you fill in your Universal Command.

Take your time. Most of your desires have already been put into motion. The Universe is weeding and sifting through all the possible mates to send your way. Being clear and specific will strengthen the signal and expedite the process by making it blatantly obvious to the Universe that there is only one man who meets all the requirements.

In creating your Universal Command, be sure to feel what you are writing as if it has just happened. You should embrace the words as an experience you are having. Be as excited, overjoyed or elated as possible, as if what you write is real and happening or happened. Feeling alters the physical world, make it feel great. There is no limit on what can come your way. The samples express stories that are in the works and will be manifest.

Enjoy the process and reach out to me with your experience. You can find the website and contact information at the back of this book. Thank you for taking the steps to empower yourself and pass it on.

"The fact is, you can't marry the best when you are dating the runner-up. When you're searching for Mr. Right, don't settle for Mr. Right Now."

Craig Groeschel

Time To Receive

You have set the wheels in motion!

Now it is time to place your Universal Order, your command that the Universe deliver exactly what you have been asking for in the exercises thus far.

Compare this next step to receiving a gift basket filled with all the goodies you can imagine, dream and think of. As if someone has been reading your mind and knows exactly what will turn you on, please you, excite you and stimulate you into joyous elation. This gift basket can be filled with things you never thought could transpire. Dream big and dream bold.

I have created a few sample Universal Commands for you, so you can see how it is done. Try to get yourself out of your own way when you fill them out. Make sure you put a date in the future.

Don't limit yourself with this process by writing *how* you will get what you are asking for. Read these three samples. Notice there is no *how* in them. Just the facts. Just the wants. Notice also that the stated desires stretch beyond what is known to be able to occur, like the New Zealand animal quarantine, the surprise sale of a home for cash, etc.

Here are three samples of the Universal Command. These will show you how to be precise and exact when filling yours out. Short and concise information is all that this needs. Like the affirmation shown in the chapter—*Create Space.* When expressing what has transpired, feel it as if it has happened and is the best news you have received in your life.

UNIVERSAL COMMAND – One

It is <u>April 30, 2017</u> and I, <u>Jane Doe</u>, currently residing at <u>1234 Main Street, Apt 567, BIG CITY, TX 77058</u> on planet Earth, have <u>just met the man I will marry. The man who I created in the *Manifest Your Mate* journal. He is a well-known landscape photographer and travels to exotic places. We are moving to New Zealand before September 12, 2017. My company has agreed to relocate me to the same city we are moving to and promoted me to a higher position with a huge salary increase. Miraculously the New Zealand government has allowed us to bring both our dogs, with no quarantine. To make it even better I just got an offer on my house for cash and they want to close within two weeks.</u>

He has <u>4 of my top 5 qualities on my list of 20 must haves</u>.

I am elated, jumping up and down with joy, happy, excited and accepting this gift...and sending an e-mail blast to my friends and family.

I give thanks to <u>my higher self, the angels, God and the mesmerizing process called life</u> for this special delivery.

It is done, it is done, it is done.... Yahoo!!!!

UNIVERSAL COMMAND – Two

It is <u>May 31, 2017</u>, and I, <u>Carol Morris</u>, residing at <u>9876 1st Street, Unit 1, SMALL CITY, AL 35004, USA</u> on planet Earth, <u>just received roses, a proposal and a huge emerald (my favorite gem) from the man I created in the *Manifest Your Mate* journal. I am meeting him tonight in Paris, France on Pont Alexandre III to say-YES.</u>

My heart is filled with joy, my body with elation and my soul with love for all.

I am grateful to the higher powers that be, God, Jesus and all the angels.

It is done, it is done, it is done----Finally!!!

UNIVERSAL COMMAND- Three

It is June 30, 2017 and I, Mary Noaj, residing at 456 78th Avenue, Bldg. 4, MIDCITY, NM, 87001, USA on planet Earth, have received an invitation, from the man I am together with the rest of life, to attend a conference in Moscow. This is the man I created in *Manifest Your Mate*. We fly there within the month and are guests of Putin for a week. I meet with Yevhen Lazarchuk, the creator of my limited-edition perfume.

I feel blessed, ecstatic, thrilled and jubilant.

I give multitudes of gratitude to the Higher Power, God, my higher self, my angels and the Universe.

It is done, it is done, it is done…. Awesome!!!

Time To Receive

This is a guideline to use as a draft to type out your own, so you have plenty of space to state what it is you have received.

UNIVERSAL COMMAND

It is _____ (full date and year you wish your desire to be fulfilled by) and I am, _____, (full birth name), currently residing at _____ (current physical address) on planet Earth .

I _____
_____
_____ The man that I created with the *Manifest a Mate* journal._____
_____
_____

He is _____ (number of qualities on list of 20 must haves) of the 20 must haves/must be on my list.

I feel _____, _____, _____. (3-4 feelings/emotions)

I am ____, _____, _____. (expressions of gratitude)

I give thanks to ____ (use your words)

It is done, it is done, it is done. ___ (your expletive)

"Destiny is no matter of chance. It is a matter of choice. It is not a thing to be waited for, it is a thing to be achieved."
William Jennings Bryan

Successes

My copy of *Manifest Your Mate* was waiting for me when I arrived home last night.

Haven't started it yet, but my wheels have been turning since our phone conversation, in regards to what kind of guy I would like to have as my partner. Already I have noticed several men have smiled at me in passing while I have been out and about. Maybe they have been there all this time and my wall is coming down, but something has definitely shifted already.

L. T., LMT- California, USA

I am now more open than I was at the beginning of the *12 Women in 12 Weeks* test group, and have had more romantic exposure-conversation in regards, even having spent the last two weeks in the mountains!

Rachel – Houston, TX

Manifest Your Mate invites us to explore our fantasies and get very specific about what we want in a mate, right down to his shoe size. The book provides space to take note of unusual encounters the reader has while doing the processes. We are coaxed to pay attention to simple events that could possibly hold deeper insight.

Three weeks into following the guidelines in the book I am convinced that the process works. There are more men paying attention to me now than have in years. I don't know how to handle all the invitations and compliments.

The sudden reality that I could have the man of my dreams in my life has frightened me a bit. Maybe I am not quite ready to be rid of my independence and autonomy. Even when I wear baggy sweaters and no make-up, they seem to just keep arriving into my life.

I just returned home from NYC where I was invited out on three dates by three different men. I went out with all of them. One of the guys meets most of the desired traits and attributes that I have listed in *Manifest Your Mate*. His eyes are a different color but perhaps that's not such a big deal. He calls every day and is planning a trip to visit me in May.

Lynne C. Robinson-publisher of taoStyle.net-Taos, NM

Within a few chapters into *Manifest Your Mate,* I noticed that I was resistant to the idea of visualizing specifics or details. I was afraid to lock myself into anything. After all, what do I care if he is blonde or not? Surely, the Universe knows better than me? But, the exercises in this workbook really did help to expand my awareness of the possibility that I might have something to do with the process of bringing my mate into my life.

Despite my initial frustrations, I did my best to continue. Strangely, a few of my exes simultaneously—*appeared*—within a week. Clearly, I was being tested on my resolve or at least reminded of what *I didn't* want—thanks for the messages, Universe!

The most notable ex was my first college love, who I had just been thinking about. He reached out to me on a social media after not talking for years!

I said. "Oh, my god! I was literally just thinking of you"

He answered, "I know! If we were 2000 miles away and connected by string, all I would have to do is tug gently on that string and you would feel it. This is me tugging on your string."

WOW! Are these the kind of signs I am supposed to look for?

Shortly after that, I dared myself to conjure up my perfect mate, as best I could. Magically, that same week, I met a gorgeous man with whom I ended up spending the entire week. Love! I thought, he must be the one! Turns out the time we spent together was just an affair because I have not heard from him since. I admit, I was miffed at first, but on reflection I understand that I had overlooked something important—*that's right*—the snarky details. His divorce wasn't final. He lives in another state. He has a few young children, and I met him late at night at a party. What was I thinking? Oops.

Now, not only am I closer to knowing myself, which is a big gift in and of itself, but I am closer to knowing how to attract my mate. Using the principles in *Manifest Your Mate,* I know I can attract the man I am meant to be with. I am excited to complete the workbook and to being more specific with my details. Now that I recognize that all those details, include upholding well defined personal boundaries, are key—*maybe the Universe won't be so confused about what it is I am looking for.*

Mary P. Shriver, LMT, TRE® - California, USA

I have so enjoyed reading your book, *Manifest Your Mate*. When you reached out to me to be one of the *12 Women in 12 Weeks* test group, the thought of imagining a new partner just kind of tickled my imagination. It was a pleasurable, sexy tickle. But five months was too soon, too scary. I was still filled with sadness after the loss of my husband, Dick, of 35 years.

I couldn't participate as needed, but I did pick it up again a few months later. As I started the process in *Manifest Your Mate*, day-by-day I found myself thinking of the possibility of finding love again. This was a quantum leap. After Dick passed, for a long time, I didn't want to live. I begged God to take me too. Life was bleak. The colors were dull.

I was surrounded by friends that wouldn't let go of me. They included and encouraged me until I found myself cautiously edging toward life again around December. Ten months had passed since my husband died and I finally felt as if I could start living again. One of these friends, and eye doctor, had a patient she thought I would like to meet. He has kind eyes and in her opinion was cute and very nice. He was a widower of two years and had lost his wife to cancer after a long happy marriage. She texted me a photo and as it appeared on my screen I noticed-he did have kind eyes. I allowed her to give him my information.

Christmas was around the corner and being home, without Dick, would be too painful. So, I decided to visit my brother for a month at his suggestion. He had called and asked for my help with daily chores. He was ill and his wife had had a stroke. I bought a one-way ticket to leave my options open and headed his way. For this entire months stay, I received texts and calls from the man with the kind eyes. We got closer to each other with a long distance between us.

One day I shared my experience of a well needed relaxing bath and a sip of wine. He didn't respond for a couple of hours. His lack of response had me wondering if he didn't drink and I'd offended him, or something had gone wrong. My next thought-*I'm surprised to find I care!* After all, this is someone I've never met. This is the same day that I was approached to edit *Manifest Your Mate*. I received the revised manuscript so I could start while I was away.

My ride home from the airport fell through. Mr. Kind Eyes offered to pick me up and take me to lunch. In *Manifest Your Mate*, I'd already planned that the first meeting of this stranger would be at a restaurant for lunch, safety's sake and to get away from him on my schedule in case the chemistry wasn't right. I told him I'd wear a red carnation and be at the passenger pickup area. That's how we met. After our month long conversations, we weren't strangers anymore.

Mr. Kind Eyes was my first kiss since losing my husband. The moment was *through the roof wonderful.* My expression of joy in sharing male companionship might have given him the wrong signal. I reread the section in *Manifest Your Mate* about rusty signals-I need to brush up on flirting again!

It's been a little over a month now and we see each other almost every day. The chemistry is amazing. I called the family together to have a ceremony to spread my husband's ashes. It was time for closure. In hospice, Dick said he wanted me to remarry. He said, "You're good at it!" He wanted me to rebuild my life, when I found the right person.

It's suddenly like the world exists in color for me. Every color, every feeling, every moment is so incredibly intense. I'm 66 years old and I thought these feelings I'm feeling were over, a bittersweet memory. Well surprise! I feel about 18.

Is this my mate? I don't know. Who marries the first guy she's kissed besides her husband in 35 years? I've told him I'll not commit at this point. He'd rather celebrate each day of this feeling and take the chance. He says that if it's meant to be, he'll be there and I'll be ready to love just him. I haven't gone out with anyone else yet, but I'm keeping that window open.

I'm so happy, so on top of the world every day. I never would have believed I'd be so happy again. Thank you, Joan, *Manifest Your Mate*, God and the universe. Life is completely changed and I'm delighted!

Barbara Szopa. Retired Teacher-Houston, TX

Afterword

By now you know, I believe we have the power to create what we want in our life. I have been the co-creator in my life too many times to think otherwise.

Back in 2005, I started taking notes and writing this journal. In 2014, I had just been speaking with my sister-in-law about writing this book and not knowing the next steps to take, as far as getting it published. I checked my e-mails and in the spam folder was an e-mail from a well-known self-publishing company. I showed it to my sister-in-law, along with the date and time stamp - it arrived during our conversation. The subject line was; *How to get your Book Published*. We both looked at each other in shock. I knew this was a message from the Universe.

I reached out to them to learn more about the process. By the time, I was ready to start actively writing and following their publishing procedure, my life took another turn, as it had so many times before. Finally, in July of 2016 I had time, was in one place for a while-I got busy.

The Universe uses all methods possible to get messages through to us. As I was doing the final edit on this book, particularly working on the Universal Command samples, my phone pinged an e-mail message alert. I quickly looked at the mail section and discovered that it was from LotusTarot.com. I have been a member of this site for years but rarely took the time to look at the emails anymore.

This one caught my eye because that morning I had received another e-mail from www.tut.com with a *Note from The Universe* in its subject. The content was reminding me with an enthusiastic tone that I am awesome and the small steps I take in any direction are applauded by the Universe. The tag line at the bottom focused my attention to the fact that I am manifesting winner.

When I opened the e-mail from LotusTarot.com, I read the first two sentences and stopped working on the Universal Commands. I took these words to heart and realized I was making Universal Commands, even though they really weren't for me. They were real to the Universe. So, I filled them out cautiously and with things that I would want to have happen in my life, just in case the Universe was going to send them in my direction.

Here is the entire e-mail:

Hi Joan,

The Magician calls on you to believe in magic!
The Magician is a card of self-realization. Power and thoughts manifest into reality. The Magician represents your inner power, the magic within you, reminding you that you are the creator of your life.

When the Magician calls, you are in the process of this creation, you remember who you are, and what you can do.

You can do anything you want; your intention is all it takes and

today you know this, today you are living in the moment and it
is delicious!

The Magician speaks to you today reminding you that you are a part of it all. You are an infinite being, experiencing life in this human form. You are remembering that you have this power, and life is falling into a sweet place, in fact it is the sweetest place you know right now. There is no fear, no doubt, in this moment you feel the love of the entire universe and you know you are on the path.

The path you are on is magical; you feel the synchronicity in every step you take. You are in the flow and it feels good! You are giving all of your attention to the present moment. This moment has become sacred, and your intention has shifted to keeping it sacred.

Everything you are doing right now, you do wholeheartedly, with everything you are. It is through this mindfulness that you are transforming, that you are shifting your life, molding it into the exact experience you want!

With the Magician comes ideas, thoughts, and solutions. You will see doors open that you did not even realize were there. The possibilities are limitless. You are pure potentiality! Be mindful of what you are creating and the process unfolds before your eyes. Stay present!

If your question today involves love, then the magician tells you that someone new is coming into your life, the love that you have been seeking is here! Open your heart and receive it! If you are in a relationship, you will find that your connection will deepen to a new place - it will be delicious!

If your question involves money or your career then relax, doors are opening in such a way that you will find deep fulfillment and financial sustainability! Listen to your inner voice, new ideas are coming through you guiding you where to go! Remember to follow your heart, and feed what excites you!

Spiritually speaking the Magician tells you that veils are lifting unlike ever before in this life, and you are connected to a deeper sense of oneness. Stay in communication with your angels, they will help you through this process. Again, relax, go with it and trust that it is taking you to a higher place. You are opening a new chapter. You are not only expanding yourself but you are helping others as well!

Stepping into the power of the Magician you feel the power of the law of giving and receiving. The universe operates in a dynamic flow, there is no end, no beginning. Energy continuously transfers. You are continuously giving and receiving energy. The more conscious you are of it, the more expanded you become; your power grows and you become lighter.

You wield the power to create what you want!

Mucho love,
Lynn Gaia
lotustarot.com

We are all in the flow and force of the Universe but only some of us are aware of it. And of those aware, fewer are aware all the time. You will know you are aware when things like the stories above happen to you and you realize, like a lightning bolt, that they are real messages

Afterword

It's as if you have been listening to one radio station all your life. You know their playlist like the back of your hand and it repeats without you even being aware anymore. Then one day, you turn on the radio and it is on an entirely different station-frequency. Your habit, has you turning it on and getting busy with your daily stuff. When suddenly you stop in your tracks when you don't hear your favorite tune. You go to the radio and are caught by what is being transmitted to you.

You hear things that are pertinent to you at that precise moment, so you sit and listen. As you listen, you know inside that the message being given to you at that moment is not by chance. Someone changed- your station- to this one, however, you are the only one living in your home.

My wish for you is: that you know when synchronistic moments are happening; that your manifesting powers become crystal clear to you; that you attract exactly what you want, when you want it. Have fun with the process and please share the secret- you are the creator of what happens in your life.

Acknowledgements

I would first like to thank all those men in my life that helped me get to the point where I am now. The ex-husbands, boyfriends and lovers. Without you my experience of what I need and want in a partner would never have been discovered. Thank you for all the good and bad times.

To my brothers whose marriages are still going strong, thank you for the proof that a marriage can last.

Thanks to all my friends and family that took me into their homes when I needed comfort, understanding and a place to stay. Your kindness and generosity is beyond compare and will never be forgotten.

Thanks to Tiba, Amelia, Monster, LuLu and Philipp Edelmann for the welcoming space to allow these words to flow.

Thanks to my Mom for allowing me to be creative in her space and grow a beautiful garden for her to play in, while we both advanced our souls.

Thanks to the twelve women who participated in the *12 Women in 12 Weeks Manifest Your Mate* test group. Your candid stories of experiences, your prompt replies and your ability to manifest, welcomed beneficial additions to this book.

I extend gratitude and admiration to my first editor, Barbara Szopa, whose expertise with the English language is something I can only dream to achieve. I realize from her efforts that I should have paid more attention in English classes throughout school.

A special thank you to Alexandra Radlovic. Having a second editor review was priceless in this first literary endeavor. Her attention to detail is beyond compare. Her dedication as a friend is priceless and my lessons in punctuation might still be needed in the future.

Thanks to Lynne C. Robinson, Cynthia Garrett, Mary Shriver Rachel T, L.T. and Barbara Szopa for allowing me to share, in this book, parts of your experiences with the process of *Manifest Your Mate*.

Thanks to all the authors of self-help books whose works awakened a fire in my soul that has led me on an amazing journey of discovery in all areas.

Thanks to Mary Oxley for all your answers and attentiveness.

Thanks to all those at Ingram Book Company for your wisdom and direction.

I am grateful for Dr. Bruce Goldberg and the special sessions we had together that quickened the printing of this book. Your advice was invaluable.

Special thanks to my Daddy, who set a very high standard for my *mate* to match up to.

References

Preface
Hashnu, O'Hara. 1910, *Concentration and the Acquirement of Personal Magnetism, Lesson 3*
http://www.psitek.net/pages/PsiTekCATAOPM5.html#gsc.tab=0 **possibly the author William Walker Atkinson.
https://en.wikipedia.org/wiki/William_Walker_Atkinson

Rauchwerger, Boaz, *31 Day Charge Program*,
http://boazpower.com

How to use this book
Welsh, Tim. June 26, 2015, originally published on TheConversation.com, http://theconversation.com/it-feels-instantaneous-but-how-long-does-it-really-take-to-think-a-thought-42392

Marriage & Commitment
Gaille, Brandon, http://brandongaille.com/25-shocking-arranged-marriages-statistics/

Afterword
Gaia, Lynn, Lotus Tarot, www.free-tarot-readings.net/card-meanings/major_arcana/the-magician/lynn

Recommended Reading

The Biology of Belief by Bruce Lipton

Love Yourself Heal your Life by Louise Hay

The Emotion Code by Dr. Bradley Nelson

I Believe by Eldon Taylor

Feelings Buried Alive Never Die by Karol K Truman

Ask and It Is Given by Esther and Jerry Hicks

The Game of Life and How to Play It by Florence Scovel Shinn

La principle du LOLA ^{2} by Rene Egli

The Holographic Universe by Michael Talbot

The Vortex by Esther and Jerry Hicks

E 2 by Pam Grout

About the Author

Joan Severance is an accomplished actress and model, inventor of the game sxTylz® and holds a Bachelor's degree in Natural Health. She is a personal empowerment coach for the *Manifest Your Mate* method. Starring in over 22 films, several T.V. series and appearing in almost every fashion magazine in the world, has allowed her to explore different places and minds on the planet. She currently resides in the USA. Read more about Ms. Severance at her website www.joanseverance.com and join in on the discussions of success with *Manifest Your Mate* at www.manifest-your-mate.com.

Social Media Links

Facebook -	joan.severance & manifestyourmate
Linkedin –	joan severance
Twitter -	@joansev
Instagram	joan_severance & manifestyourmate
Websites	joanseverance.com & manifest-your-mate.com

CPSIA information can be obtained
at www.ICGtesting.com
Printed in the USA
FFOW03n1305101017
40949FF